FROM
FANTASY TRUST
TO
REAL TRUST

LEARNING FROM OUR
DISAPPOINTMENTS AND BETRAYALS

Other Books by the authors:
-Face to Face With Fear – Transforming Fear Into Love
Perfect Publishers 2009
-Stepping Out of Fear – Breaking Free of Pain and Suffering
Langdon Street Press, 2009
-When Sex Becomes Intimate – How Sexuality Changes As Your Relationship
Deepens
Strategic Book Publishing, 2008

ISBN-10: 1461000947
EAN-13: 9781461000945

FROM
FANTASY TRUST
TO
REAL TRUST

LEARNING FROM OUR
DISAPPOINTMENTS AND BETRAYALS

KRISHNANANDA TROBE, M.D.
AND AMANA TROBE

TABLE OF CONTENTS

DEDICATION:

We would like to dedicate this book to all couples who undertake and sustain the challenge of the journey of love.

⟡

For Information about The Learning Love Institute and the work of Krishnananda and Amana:

Learning Love Institute, LLC
Krishnananda and Amana,
Founders and Directors
750 Sunshine Lane
Sedona, AZ 86336 USA
Tel: 1 928 203 0966
Email: info@learningloveinstitute.com
Web site: www.learningloveinstitute.com

Cover Painting, "Safe Passage" by Michael Colpitts, Sedona, 2007
www.artfulceramics.com

Cover Design by Anugito, Sedona, AZ, USA 2007 www.artlinegraphics.com

INTRODUCTION:

RECOVERING THE TRUST WE LOST

T here seems to be no greater issue in life than trust. We have learned and continue to learn lessons about trust all the time; when we go through difficult times in our life, our trust is tested. We felt motivated to write a book about trust because after many years of self-work and ongoing work with others in seminars and individual sessions, trust seems to be one of the most vital issues we all face.

We have been together as a couple for nearly eighteen years and have been working together since 1995. What we are teaching now is both a product of our togetherness and what we have learned from working with others. This book has been a joint effort. We would sit with a chapter after we had written it, keep feeling and rewriting until we felt that it worked and was what we wanted to say. In the process of writing, which took over two years, we have also had to deal with different issues that came up between us—very much a part of what we were writing about. This beautiful process has drawn us closer together and made us more trusting of each other.

Our quality of trust is measured by the state of our life—by the love we feel for ourselves, by the depth of intimacy we have with those close to us, and by the joy with which we approach life. Developing a quality of mature trust is the pot of gold at the end of the rainbow of inner work. We can do endless therapy on discovering our childhood wounds but if it does not lead us to a greater level of genuine trustfulness then what is the point? Something will be deeply missing. However, we need some tools in order to use the challenging experiences in our life—the curveballs that existence throws us—to open rather than close our hearts.

Very often, when we get hurt, we have a tendency to shut down to the person or people who hurt us and in that way, we shut down to ourselves and to our connection to the universe. This shutting down is very painful, even though we may not feel the pain, and it is the root cause of many diseases, both physical and psychological. When we shut down, we retreat into a place of profound mistrust and see life and people from this space of mistrust. We are like a wounded animal in a cave looking out suspiciously at the world. From this place, it is impossible to clearly see the people in our life and, because of this, we often overreact or push them away not to get hurt again.

When we are like this wounded animal in our mistrust cave, we tend to recycle the same negative thoughts and beliefs repeatedly. We may become accustomed to living in blame and isolation. We live in a painful cycle of hoping to be treated in a certain way so that we can feel safe to come out of our cave but when our expectations are disappointed, as they inevitably are, we retreat into our cave, fully believing in the truth of our mistrust. We then brood in solitude and create all kinds of reasons not to engage in the life of people. When we feel lonely and unnourished in our cave, we may try again to come out—hoping that life and people will make it safe for us this time.

This approach to life is problematic. Not only do we rely on outside treatment to renew our trust, we also become accustomed to believing that our nourishment in life is dependent on outer events and that our nourishment in relationships is dependent on how other people behave with us. This way of being with life and ourselves, creates bitterness and anger and does not help us to learn and grow into trusting individuals.

We need a framework, an understanding, to help us recognize the value of disappointments and pain so that they can actually give us strength rather than weaken and destroy our trust in people and in life.

The understanding that is needed is:

Pain and disappointment challenge us to discover real trust and this process is a journey. When we see the spiritual and emotional meaning to our difficult times, it is easier to feel the pain and grow from experiences that trigger our mistrust.

Lacking this understanding, our hurts can easily become terrifying and unbearable. Perhaps we take for granted that it is not possible to trust or perhaps we have openings and trustful experiences and then something happens that closes us. We may alternate between times of feeling blissfully trusting in another person or in life in general and other times of feeling separate and isolated.

The quality of genuine trustfulness is not, as we might believe it to be, dependent on other people or anything on the outside. Rather it is a deep inner experience of feeling connected to our being and to existence. Our level of genuine trustfulness, one that is not dependent on outside events, is a direct mirror of our consciousness. Genuine trustfulness is a quality that we can develop. We are not as helpless as it might seem when it comes to opening our hearts to life, to others, and ultimately to ourselves, because, fundamentally, others are not who we need to learn to trust again;

it is ourselves. We have lost trust because, along the way, we never learned the basic tools for trusting ourselves—our intuition, our thoughts and feelings, and our ability to distinguish between what we need and want from another or from life and what does not feel right.

In subsequent chapters, we take up specific aspects of how we develop genuine trustfulness. Most of us now are not living in trust. If we experience a feeling of trustfulness, it is actually what we call "fantasy trust," not real trust. Fantasy trust is built on *expectations and beliefs* of how life, existence (or God), and others should be and should treat us. Naturally, when those expectations are not met, we become mistrustful and we build rage, resentment, and resignation. Furthermore, we can easily feel victimized by how people and life are treating us.

There is a part of us inside which lives in fantasy trust and perhaps will do so forever. It is a young, naive and wounded inner space that needs our understanding and our love. When we are hurt, this part of us holds on to resentment with a formidable tenacity. But this is not by any means all of who we are. Another aspect of our consciousness is deeper and wiser. This part can help us to gently turn away from expectations, blame, and negativity toward deeper responsibility. It can teach us to welcome disappointments and frustrations as opportunities to deepen, grow, and mature. It can guide us to see that life is actually loving and benevolent. And we come to see and feel the real beauty in life and in the people close to us—in our lover, our friends, our children, and our parents.

* * *

PART 1:

WHAT IS TRUST?

CHAPTER 1:

TESTS OF TRUST –

Learning to Integrate Frustration, Disappointment, and Betrayal

Consciousness is painful,
because you will have to uncover your wounds
which you have covered and completely forgotten.
You will have to revive all worries and anguishes
that somehow you have repressed.
Osho

We carry inside of us a wound of betrayal. And our heart and body hold the experience of this betrayal. However, often we are not aware of this experience and we are not aware of the ways it affects our life today. But when life presents us with frustrating and disturbing experiences that are sometimes deeply painful and devastating, it reawakens this wound of betrayal. Often, these disappointments occur when our expectations are not met. Sometimes, they come in the form of feeling betrayed or deceived by someone we loved and trusted. Sometimes, they occur when we feel that someone abused his or her power over us.

An acquaintance of ours was in a twelve-year relationship with a man whom she felt was the love of her life. He had a passion for sailing and wanted to take three years to sail around the world. Although she did not particularly enjoy sailing, she did not want to be away from him for such a long time and agreed to leave the life they were living and accompany him on this journey. She soon began to hate living on the small space of the boat. During this time they grew apart and eventually split up. Most likely, other factors about their relationship contributed to their separation but she is convinced that their relationship ended because he talked her into taking this trip and she allowed herself to be talked into it. She now would like to start a new relationship but she is still resentful toward her husband for putting his own needs above the relationship and she is angry with herself for betraying her own needs. She cannot yet see that her breakup was anything more than a bad experience.

Another acquaintance of ours fell deeply in love with a woman and after years of being alone, he finally felt he had found the woman of his life. As he got to know her, he realized that she was an alcoholic—something she had hidden from him. He had also not seen that she was irresponsible in the way she dealt with life and other people. Slowly her drinking became more and more obvious, but not before she had convinced him to pay for remodeling her home. He felt utterly betrayed. In the hope that he finally had found intimacy and someone to take him out of his loneliness, he could not see what he was getting himself into. It was a rude and totally unexpected awakening for him that she was not the person he thought she was.

I (Krish) remember feeling deeply betrayed by a therapist years ago. I was in a counseling training program and part of the program was to participate in a group with one of the therapists on staff. During the group, she invited me to come up in front of the room with another participant and asked me to work with this person in front of the group. Her way of teaching was to point out that what I was doing was precisely the wrong way of doing therapy; that I had no "resonance," as she called it, no ability to take in the person, and no deeper appreciation for the subtleties of working with people. Perhaps this was sincerely the way she thought it was best to teach, but I felt ridiculed and put down in front of the group and, for a long time afterward, I was hurt, resentful, and reluctant to expose myself in similar situations. I was furious at her for abusing me and furious at myself for not standing up for myself.

Common Responses to Betrayal

The most common way that we deal with such experiences is to **deny** that we have been hurt. Pretending that we are not disturbed was an effective way of coping with disappointment and betrayal early in life and we often continue to behave the same way. But, denial doesn't make the hurt go away nor does it give us the space to process and grow from the hurt. Furthermore, when we deny something, we become irritable, moody, and resentful and we withdraw from the person who hurt us. *This kind of reaction indicates that something is disturbed inside—something we need to look at.*

The next most common way of reacting to frustration, disappointment, and betrayal is to go into **resignation**. We feel let down, and inside we say to ourselves, "What is the use of staying open, of trusting anyone, or even of showing our hurt because they don't understand or care anyway." Or we may escape into a spiritual concept to deaden the pain and disappointment, saying things like, "I should be evolved enough to handle this." "Anger and hurt is not very mature." "I obviously am creating this for my own good."And so on. But resignation or escaping into pseudo-spiritual concepts is no more helpful than denial and has the added poison of dampening our life energy and our joy.

Finally, a third way of dealing with a betrayal experience is with **blame, resentment, and bitterness** toward the person or situation that provoked it. Many of us may even be familiar with holding on to resentful feelings for years. It can lead us to become cynical about life and people in general. This anger that we harbor inside is unhealthy and we may find ourselves becoming judgmental and critical of others as a way of diffusing our anger indirectly. All of these reactions are natural and predictable but if we don't take it further than that, we don't grow from the experiences. Instead, we stay victimized; our mistrust grows and festers inside; and, most likely, we will continue to repeat the same situations.

Our wound of betrayal may have different inner voices (which we usually are not aware of). It can be:

"I feel not supported."
"I feel unloved."
"I feel mistreated, abused, or deceived."
"No one understands me."
"I feel ignored."
"I feel left out."
"This world is not a safe place."
"I am too sensitive for this world."

> *We may be unaware that our betrayal wound has its roots in childhood and are often unaware how it still operates in our life today. Now, when we have an experience of disappointment, frustration, and betrayal, it activates our wound of betrayal that comes from our past. But we often put all the blame and responsibility on the person or event today.*

Betrayal Experiences Kick Us up the Ladder of Consciousness

The emotions that arise inside of us when we feel ongoing frustration with someone or when we feel deeply disappointed and betrayed are powerful. This energy is wonderful and it is vital not to repress or dampen it in any way. It is important to allow ourselves to feel the intensity of emotion that these experiences provoke. But we can't stop there. We need to integrate and work through them and for that we need tools. These experiences are building blocks for our inner growth.

Recently, we were doing a session with a person in Byron Bay, Australia. He was devastated because his wife had left him some months before, taking their two children with her. He told us that for much of the thirteen years they had been together, they had fought even over the smallest things. Now, he was feeling deep remorse at how disturbed he had been about details, how he had needed to be right all the time, how he had questioned her judgment incessantly, and in general, how he had treated her without love and respect. He was also seeing that he demonstrated the same impatience and criticalness toward his subordinates at work that he had toward his wife. He was extremely hard on them when they made mistakes and exacted such high standards for them that he frightened them most of the time.

He also told us that since he was six, he had spent most afternoons after school working with his father who, for as long as he could remember, struggled to make a living and finally ended up going bankrupt. His father put strong pressure on him to work hard and be proficient even though he himself felt like a failure in life. We helped him to see that the pressure he put on others was a mirror of the pressure he put on himself, which covered a deep fear of ending up a failure like his father. His wife's leaving him had opened him to looking into himself in a way that he had never done before. He was going to counseling regularly; he was developing a relationship with his mother and his sister that was warmer and deeper than he had had before; he was learning to be gentler with people at work; and he was crying for the first time in his life.

I (Amana) went through a very intensely painful experience when I was twenty-two years old. Up until that point, I had always been good at everything I did and never had any failures. At age twenty-two, I decided to become a journalist. After having traveled a lot, I felt it was time for an education and this was what appealed to me. I took the exams to enter and didn't make it into the school. This was a huge blow to my ego and I went into complete shock. I was used to being the first in my class, and the idea that someone could reject me because I was not good enough was totally beyond my imagination.

Yet this rejection opened me up to deeper places inside. Suddenly I was in a black hole of feeling worthless, full of shame, and feeling like a failure. This was the first time I saw my limitations. It was painful but also very healthy. I am grateful now that this happened to me. I don't know what kind of person I would have become if I had been accepted into the school. This rejection made me human for the first time, and it opened up my feelings. I remember lying on the bed for hours crying. This was the first time I had cried since I was a child. I had closed down so completely that nothing would get through to me, and I was used to getting my way. I was sobbing, feeling like I was going to die, and in so much shame that I wasn't able to face the world. My heart was aching as if it was breaking.

At the time, I didn't know what was happening but, looking back, I can see that I was touching my core of worthlessness. I stayed with the pain and slowly it began to ease. Shortly afterward, I met my spiritual teacher and started meditating. Something that I had not consciously been looking for started happening on its own and it feels like this failure, combined with the fact that I went so deeply into the pain of it, was like an initiation into my inner world.

Disturbance, disappointments, and betrayals provide the friction for growth. It kicks us up the ladder of consciousness.

These experiences are life's way of waking us up, letting us know that there is inner work to do, deepening us and making us human. When we know that there is a deeper significance to being frustrated, disturbed or in pain, it gives us the motivation to work with these experiences.

Shortly after graduating from college, a woman I (Krish) had been with for three years in college left me. I went into a space of such intense fear, loneliness, and confusion that for some months, I was unable to function. Furthermore, I could not understand why all of this was happening. We had been pulling away from each other for a year before we actually split up and it was clear to both of us that it wasn't working anymore. So why was I feeling so much pain? The pain lasted off and on for over three years. I thought it would never end and, at times, it felt like I couldn't bear it. (At that time, I knew nothing about the abandonment wound.)

When I recovered from the depression and the panic, I continued to ruminate ceaselessly about what I had done wrong or on how I could get her back. I drove people close to me crazy with my endless ruminating and self-pity. But something changed inside of me because of that time. I deepened. I found a reservoir inside where I knew, in some unexplainable way, that I could handle anything. It was as though I had fallen as deeply as I could fall and found a space where I could rest and feel held. Also, I began to see the world differently, less naïvely and more compassionately. I woke up from a dream of living life like a robot following the script I had been given, focused on achievement and repressing uncomfortable feelings of any kind. Since then, similar experiences of loss have been much easier to get through. (Once we survive our first abandonment experience, later ones seem to be easier, perhaps just as painful initially, but less overwhelming, and we recover more quickly.)

> *Betrayal experiences can shatter us. They can shatter our efforts to keep life under control. They can shatter our ideas of what life is about. They can shatter our small-minded ego*

that would like to understand everything. They can force us to confront our deepest doubts and mistrust in life and to face the fear that we are not cared for or held by existence. There is a part of us inside that trembles all the time and often for no clear reason. This part of us carries profound fears that things will not work out, fears about whether we will have security, safety, survival, and love.

We can deny that we have this terrified part of us inside and we can spend a great deal of energy trying to keep everything in control so we don't have to feel this incredible fear. Betrayal experiences expose our fears and reveal how little we trust. They are life's way of helping us develop real trust, a trust that cannot be destroyed by life's adversities.

Exercise:

Recall some experiences from your childhood that damaged your trust in yourself or others.

Ask yourself:

1. *What beliefs did I develop due to these experiences?*

2. *How have these experiences affected my life in terms of my trust in myself, my self-confidence, and my intimate relating?*

* * *

CHAPTER 2:

TWO KINDS OF TRUST –

Fantasy Trust and Real Trust

People who trust themselves can trust others.
People who don't trust themselves cannot trust anybody.
Out of self-trust, trust arises.
Because if you don't trust yourself,
how can you trust your trust.
Osho

In a recent workshop we did, a woman shared that in her relationship with her husband, she felt deeply insecure because she felt that he felt attractions for other women and she was never sure whether she could trust him. She asked him repeatedly if he was having affairs with other women and he continually denied it. But she still felt insecure and somehow could not believe him. When she returned from the workshop, she found that he had been with another woman and that the relationship had been going on for some time. Furthermore, he told her that he no longer wanted to be with her. She felt utterly betrayed and felt that now she could no longer trust any man ever again.

While we supported her to feel the anger and hurt that this situation was bringing up for her, we explained that what she had been calling trust was not trust at all but a fantasy of her hopes. This experience, although deeply painful, was in some way a gift because it was shattering her fantasies and helping her to trust herself. She had been feeling all along that he was not there for her, but didn't trust her own feelings, choosing instead to listen to his "reassuring" words. What she was calling "trust" was what we call "fantasy trust." Her experience was actually helping her to break out of this kind of trust and discover real trust. It was helping her to ground herself in her own feelings and have the courage to see things and other people exactly as they are, not how she wanted them to be. Sometimes it can be very painful to wake up from our fantasies.

Fantasy Trust and Global Mistrust

Fantasy trust depends on how we are treated—by others and by the world in general. We "trust" someone when he or she treats us as we feel we should be treated or according to how we believe one should treat another person. We "trust" someone when he or she lives up to our expectations. And when someone invades us or hurts us, we don't "trust" him (or her) anymore. This kind of trust is not really trust because it is dependent on outside factors. However this is usually what we mean when we use the word "trust." When we say, "I trust you" or "I trust that person," we usually mean, "he or she has treated us in a way that makes us feel trusting." But most of the time, we have not really taken the person in. We have not seen the person clearly, which means that eventually, he or she will probably do something that destroys our "trust." And with accumulated betrayals and invasions, we stop trusting others as a whole even if we develop a mask of "trust" or "openness." Most of us live either in a state of fantasy trust or global mistrust.

Ordinarily, our idea of mistrust is as unconscious as our concept of trust. Often, when we feel mistrust for someone, it is an emotional reaction, not a mature response. When someone does or says something that makes us feel mistrustful, it triggers a space inside that was already deeply wounded and mistrustful. It has opened our mistrust bank, which has been receiving deposits for a very long time. We call this kind of mistrust "global mistrust" because it is not discriminating, objective, or clear. Our history of betrayal and invasion, which strongly colors how we experience the present, emotionally contaminates it. Unconscious memories of being invaded and betrayed in the past, especially as a child, are awakened when we are triggered.

Our mistrust formed at the time of these traumas and it became frozen in time. It lurks in the basement of our consciousness, awaiting provocations in our life today. These provocations can come from lovers, friends, authority figures, children, or parents—in short, anyone with whom we invest our energy, anyone who is significant to us in some way. Simple events in life can also provoke us. And in the moment when our mistrust is provoked, we feel not only the betrayal in the present but all the accumulated betrayals of the past. Our mistrust can be so strong that it can sabotage relationships or work situations. We want to hold on to our fantasies and each new betrayal simply adds to our growing list of deceptions.

For instance, I (Krish) get very disturbed when someone is unreliable and inconsiderate with me. In my fantasy trust, I imagine that the world *should* be a place where people are responsible and considerate with each other. I have a childish resistance to letting go of the belief that people should do what they say they are going to do and treat others (meaning me) with respect. (Not that I always do that, by any means.) Lurking under my fantasy trust is a deep conviction (my global mistrust) that people are not going to treat me the way I expect them to. When they don't, I feel that my whole world has fallen apart and I am furious for being deceived and betrayed once again.

Some years ago, I purchased a used scooter from a merchant in the town in which we live. I paid the money and got a bill of sale but the person who sold me the vehicle told me that it would take a little while for him to get me the title. I never feel very comfortable dealing in the world of cars and such things and easily get intimidated. So without asking for specifics, I left, naively assuming that in a few days, he would give me the title. It took me three weeks to get that damn title and that was only after I had made many phone calls, most of which were not returned and after exploding in his office (that was before I learned "Non-Violent Communication."). This incident directly confronted me with my fantasy trust—of not wanting to let go of the idea that the world is a safe and loving place where it is always safe to trust and be vulnerable. I had no doubt that my reaction was the result of all prior times of feeling disrespected and my unwillingness to let go of my fantasies.

The Pendulum of Resignation and Hope

When we live in fantasy trust, we swing between feeling hope and despair. When we enter into a new relationship or life situation, we may approach it full of positive expectations and openness. But just like a child, we enter into these situations blindly. Then we get disappointed and become enraged or resigned; our hope fizzles, and gets replaced with a hopeless feeling that it is not possible to trust anyone ever. We may start the cycle repeatedly, each time with the same childish hope followed by the same blanket of despair. After a while, we may even become jaded, cynical, and lifeless. In our fantasy state, we believe, just like a small child, that someone or something from the outside is going to make us happy.

> *To come out of despair, resentment, resignation, bitterness, and blame, we have to find a new way of relating to life and people—a way that takes into consideration the fact that at times we are not going to be treated as we feel is right and fair. We need to find a new way of*

relating to life experiences that are painful and sometimes brutally disappointing. In short, we have to make some sense out of what has happened to us and continues to happen that closed or closes our heart and make sense out of experiences that may bring disappointment.

Paradoxically, these disappointments help us to mature and grow out of our fantasy trust. Without them, we would remain in a childish state of idealizations and hopes. There is a huge leap in consciousness from expecting life and people to treat us a certain way and growing mistrustful when they don't, to experiencing that life is deeply nourishing exactly as it is even if at times, it brings sadness, pain, and disappointment. That is the journey of discovering real trust.

Real Trust

Real trust is based on a deep inner experience that we are being held and cared for by existence. It is based on an inner knowing that the experiences that come to us, whether positive or negative, pleasant or painful, are an integral part of our growth as human beings. It is also a deep inner knowing that by not fighting with the pain that life invariably brings, these experiences take us to higher levels of maturity. With this kind of trust inside, we can recover from even the most painful of setbacks, failures, and rejections and are able to pick ourselves up again and keep going with a positive attitude toward life.

Fundamentally, this kind of trust is not dependent on how well or how badly others and the world treat us. It is a quality deep inside that remains untouched by the outside. Most of us don't have this kind of trust. As children, we had a precious innocence and trustfulness but it was as yet untested, and over the years most of us lost touch with this innocence. Yet, the naïve trust that we all had as children has the potential to become transformed into mature real trust. From our experience, no matter how traumatic our childhoods may have been, we can develop this kind of mature trust with sincere inner work.

When we have real trust inside, it does not mean that we never mistrust. But our mistrust is a response in the here and now toward a person or situation based on what we observe clearly and unemotionally. We may conclude, according to what we see and feel and experience from a person (or situation), that it does not feel safe enough or appropriate for us to entrust our vulnerability. It is as simple as that. There is no need for us to react or be upset about the other person's behavior because we understand that there are no guarantees when we open up to someone. It is a decision made from clarity and acceptance for how things are, not as how we would like them to be. This kind of clear perception allows us to discriminate and to open when we feel safe and received, or to stay closed when we feel that is appropriate in the situation. Seeing the situation as it is. Furthermore, when we are grounded in trust, if someone mistreats us or deceives us, it is much easier to isolate our mistrust to that specific situation rather than having it affect our whole attitude toward people or life.

The Transition from Fantasy to Reality

Why is it so hard to trust our intuition? Why is it so hard to extract ourselves from a situation that is unnourishing or even harmful and threatening? Many times, some deep inner sense is signaling to us, saying, "Watch out, get out, something is not right here, don't go into this!" But we don't listen. Why instead do we hope for the best and often discover the worst? Because we are so hungry for love and so shocked in our feelings and intuition that we are not present enough to hear our inner voice of wisdom.

I (Krish) was recently working with a woman who told me that she had been married for twenty years to a man who was a "rageaholic" just like her father. When I asked her why she stayed with him, she said, "I guess I was so hungry for love and attention that I took the first man who told me that he loved me. I stayed because I believed that I would never find anyone else. And I was much too scared to stand up to him and tell him that I didn't like it when he screamed at me."

I (Amana) have been working intensively with a woman who is repeatedly with men who are unavailable, sexually aggressive, and generally invasive and disrespectful. She was sexually abused by her father and emotionally abused by her mother. She feels so terrified of men, so insecure about herself, and so hungry for any kind of attention and love, that she will settle for whatever she can get. Furthermore, she doesn't even imagine that she could say or even feel what she wants and needs, let alone set a limit or express herself. Now, after a lot of work, she is beginning to set limits and have the courage to stay alone rather than being in an abusive relationship. She is even beginning to enjoy her alone time.

We are too traumatized to trust our intuition. Many of us are far too buried in disappointments and betrayals to open our hearts again and too buried in shame and self-doubt to trust ourselves.

> *The process of learning to trust others and ourselves again is a journey. It begins with discovering how and why we lost it and feeling the pain and grief. We also need to develop deep compassion for the traumas we have been through. Then there are specific lessons to learn and apply in our life today that continues the journey of recovery. We will present and explore these lessons in later chapters.*

We rediscover real trust by beginning to trust ourselves again. Life, existence, or God (whatever word we like to use) seems determined to wake us up out of our fantasies. It continues to present us with situations that shatter our hopes and expectations in order to help us open our eyes and see life as it is. But we need the understanding and tools to make sense and grow from these shattering experiences.

A German woman who participated in one of our seminars had left a booming practice as a health care practitioner in Germany to live with her American husband in the United States. From living a life of success and creativity, she suddenly found herself in a new and strange environment doing menial work to make a living. Her husband was not giving her the support and nurturing she wanted and they were fighting much of the time. This person had been working on herself for many years with intensive therapy workshops and meditation. Yet by making this move to America, she was coming up against one of her deepest fantasies and hopes—that of being taken care of by a man who is fully attentive to her needs and who would even relieve her of the need to struggle for survival. Deep inside, she was hoping that her husband would give her what she never got as a child—a deep sense of feeling safe and cared for. She was not getting that from him and she was enraged.

It seemed to us as we heard the story and got to know her that she was ready to receive this strong life lesson even though it was painful and shattering. She was ready to begin letting go of the hope and expectation that a man would fill the emptiness from her painful childhood and instead to seek the nurturing inside herself. She was ready to begin to see what her husband *was* giving her, instead of focusing on what was missing. Her husband actually loved her in his own way but her expectations prevented her from seeing and receiving that love and she was even pushing him away.

Perhaps a part of us never stops hoping and continues to feel enraged when our hopes are shattered. But we can arrive at a point where that part of us stops leading our life and controlling our consciousness. Once we begin to understand the difference between fantasy trust and real trust, we can recognize when our fantasies have taken over, and that awareness gives us space to see the reality of the situation. It is a bit like taking off rose-colored glasses and seeing things as they are. Even though it might be painful to see things clearly, ultimately, it is much more nourishing to face reality rather than living in fantasy.

Exercise:

Recall the most recent times that you felt let down or betrayed by someone important to you.

Ask yourself:

1. *Did I get signals earlier that would have alerted me to expect this kind of behavior from this person?*

2. *Why did I not listen to those signals? What was I wanting that made it difficult for me to see reality and made me unable to trust myself?*

* * *

CHAPTER 3:

REMOVING THE VEIL OF ILLUSION –

Trading Childish Innocence for Humanness and Depth

You go on missing something –
something that you had known but you have forgotten,
a faded memory, a lost remembrance.
And the gap is not only a gap, it is a wound,
because you have brought something with your birth into the world
And you have lost it somewhere.
This is the greatest crime that is committed against every child.
To spoil a child's trust is to spoil his whole life
because trust is so valuable that the moment you lose trust,
you lose your contact with your own being.
Osho

We are often asked, "When is the inner emotional work over?" Our response is that the work is not over as long as we are still living in fantasy trust or in global mistrust. This will show itself in our life today—in our feeling disappointed and betrayed by friends and lovers, in our difficulties in love and intimacy, in judgments of ourselves and others, in the ways that the flow of our life energy is blocked, and in our depression and resignation.

> *As long as our present is still affected in a negative way by our past and as long as we have not deeply embraced our fears and insecurities without judgment or preference, there is more to explore, feel, and understand.*

By "emotional work," we do not mean continual primal work, although that too is important and much-needed work. (By primal work, we mean exploring childhood wounds by regressing back to earlier times with the resources and awareness of an adult.) Nor do we mean becoming identified with our past and our wounds to the point of using them as an excuse not to risk or live with integrity. We mean a willingness to investigate and feel our emotional reactions to events in our life today. And because the way we react to these current situations is strongly influenced by earlier traumatic events, it is important to see and feel the connection between the past and the present.

> *The past does not truly become the past until it no longer influences our present.*

Coming Out of Denial

One significant aspect of doing emotional work is to come out of denial. Some of us have a compelling and persistent need to hold on to our illusions, particularly about the past. It is common to minimize the impact of our past traumas for many reasons. We all learned to survive one way or another and in doing so, we often bury the ways our trust was damaged and even the memories of how this happened. Furthermore, we get on with our lives without realizing how our present life is profoundly affected by what happened long ago. Our past traumas are very deep and we have much to learn from taking the time and care to uncover the truth of how our innocence was damaged. Every one of us has had our innocence betrayed in one way or another and if we make the effort to work through our betrayal, we trade our childish innocence for something immensely more valuable. We learn to become profoundly human.

Recently, a close friend of mine (Krish) and I were playing tennis at our local tennis club in Sedona where we live. Across from us was a father teaching his son to play. The son must have been no older than six. The father's methods of instruction were to berate the child continually—for not trying hard enough, not putting enough topspin on the ball, not putting enough energy into his shots, not using proper footwork, not changing his grip from forehand to backhand, not stepping into the ball, and so on. The child was complaining that he was not feeling well (which was probably the only way that he could deal with the situation).

I suspect that the father's intentions were good; he sincerely wanted to teach his son to play and to share with him the passion and enjoyment that he has derived from the game. And he was probably doing to his son what his father had done to him. Perhaps, he still believes that this is how to teach. My friend and I both observed the situation before we spoke to each other about it. (We are both therapists and do much the same kind of work.) When we stopped to drink some water, we both acknowledged that we were aware of what was going on in the next court and recognized that we have been working through conditioning that was not much different from what this boy was receiving.

There is another reason that it is difficult to recover our trust. Many of us are schooled with the idea that we need to forgive those who traumatized us. But "forgiveness" is often grossly misunderstood. It can easily motivate us to skip over truly feeling and understanding the impact that our traumas had on us and continue to exert on our lives. Furthermore, forgiveness is not something that we do, it is something that naturally happens once we have deeply processed and integrated our wounds. Only then can we look to those who raised us and understand that they did the best that they could given the consciousness that they had.

When we relive our past trauma with the awareness and resources of an adult, we can appreciate why our mistrust is so deep. We can also appreciate why we are dysfunctional in some areas of our life. We start to develop compassion and understanding for our current fears and insecurities when we *feel* what happened to us. It is difficult to understand how mistrust and dysfunction develop unless we take an honest and naked look at what we went through children and feel these experiences from the perspective of a helpless and undefended child (but with the bird's-eye view of an adult). It may often be difficult to remember and clearly see what happened to us as children. However, we can observe how mistrustful we are today and slowly piece together the story of where this state of mistrust came from and how it developed.

Recognizing the Depth of Our Mistrust

We do an exercise in our workshops as part of our work with mistrust. We ask people to pick a partner and stand facing each other. We invite one person to imagine that he or she is removing the layer of protection that surrounds him or her and, with open eyes, slowly come closer to the other person totally naked and vulnerable without knowing if the other person is vulnerable and receptive or closed. At a certain point, we ask the person to verbalize the fears that come up as he or she comes closer to the other person without protection. This simple exercise helps people to see how afraid and mistrustful they actually are underneath their protections.

Most of us have developed a cellular belief that if we let down our defenses something terrible will happen to us or we might do something terrible ourselves. This deeply rooted belief even affects our nervous system in irrational and unpredictable ways so that the fear can make us unable to function. This may occur in sex, in allowing another to come close, in expressing our creativity, confronting or attempting to be honest with another, allowing ourselves to have joy and pleasure, feeling our emotions or our body, or even in unexplainable attacks of panic. It can also show itself in difficulties sleeping or in other body symptoms. Often, no amount of encouragement from the inside or from others makes any difference. We are gripped by mistrust and fear.

Some of our traumas came from repetitive disrespects and invasions. We call these "invasion traumas." For instance, we may have been disciplined in harsh and unloving ways, watched our parents fighting, or experienced one of our parents being violent or angry. Perhaps a parent commonly told us what to do, what to think, what to wear, how to behave, what to feel without tuning into us, communicating in a loving way, or making an effort to understand and feel us.

We may also have had what we call "abandonment traumas" such as feeling the physical or emotional absence of one or both parents, or feeling a lack of attunement, appreciation, or attention. Some of our traumas were simply accidental such as an illness or an accident, being left alone in the hospital, or the death or absence of a parent at an early age. Often these traumas profoundly affect how we relate to the world, to others and to ourselves. It is important to penetrate them deeply.

As an infant, I (Krish) had neonatal malabsorption syndrome and during the first days of my life, my mother sat by my hospital bed without knowing if I would survive. (I did.) Years later, I reviewed this experience through various types of inner work and recognized that from those early moments, I formed a powerful symbiotic bond with my mother who was my link between life and death. That bond has not been easy to separate from and resulted in difficulties with my subsequent relationships with women. Also, because of my father's work with Jewish refugees, we moved every three or four years from one city in Europe to another, forcing me to leave school and friends, and relocate in a totally new environment. At the time, I never considered that these moves were traumatic but now I see that I am numb whenever I leave someone or some place.

When I was seven, I (Amana) was abruptly taken away from my father, my friends, my toys and the house I lived in, when one day, my mother packed the car and took me and my brother away from my father. My father was an alcoholic. I remember having felt the tension and fear in the house for a long time. My mother never knew when or if he would come home from work. He would disappear for days and weeks at a time whenever he received his paycheck. His behavior was totally unpredictable. When he was home, he was sweet, loving, playful, and attentive, but when he would drink, he became another person—depressive, irresponsible, and sometimes violent. After we left, it was a year before my brother and I were allowed to see him every other weekend. His behavior became more and more self-destructive and when I was eighteen, his drinking killed him.

Over time, I came to understand how great my trauma was. I absorbed my mother's fears of survival and at the same time, I lost my father whom I loved very deeply. Even today, after having worked with this for many years, I still notice how any changes in plans unsettle me and it takes time for me to adjust. Looking back at this situation today, I am deeply grateful that my mother had the courage and strength to take us away and create a much better life for her and for my brother and me. But at the time, it felt like a deep betrayal to be taken away from my father and not being allowed to see him at all the first years after the divorce. I felt guilty and conflicted for loving him. For many years I pretended that I didn't need a father and it wasn't until many years later in therapy that I was able to allow myself to feel and express how much I loved and missed him. By then he had already been dead many years, but it was a deep healing for me to allow the feelings of love and pain of not having had a father.

There Are Many Causes of Mistrust

For most of us, our childhood is a mix of positive and negative experiences. Often, though, we remember the good and forget the negative. That is natural because we may be reluctant to say or even think anything negative about our parents but it prevents us from understanding where the depth of our mistrust comes from.

Recently, I (Krish) was working with a man whose father had repeatedly yelled at and beaten his mother and beaten the children. When I asked him how it felt being raised by a violent father, he objected vehemently to my labeling his father as "violent."

"I love my father," he said, "and I think he was doing the best he could. After all, he was living under a lot of stress."

"Of course, I don't want you to blame your father but, I wonder, what do you think it is like for a child who is raised in an environment where his father is beating his wife and sometimes slapping him as well?" I asked.

He suddenly began to cry, recalling an incident in his own family when he and his wife were fighting and his five-year-old daughter began to cry. In between his tears, he told me that he could see the fear in his daughter's eyes.

"Oh, my gosh," he said, "I never want her to experience that again!"

"Perhaps, then," I added after a pause, "you can appreciate what it must have been like for you."

Later in the session, he was also able to see how profoundly his father's behavior and temperament had influenced his being overly strict and disciplinarian with his children and tyrannical with his wife.

To some extent, the ways in which we felt unloved, unappreciated, unseen, disrespected, or even abused may seem insignificant because, for most of us, they were the bread and butter of our upbringing. But to a sensitive child, they are devastating. These do not necessarily need to come from flagrant abuses such as physical, sexual, or reoccurring emotional abuse. Naturally such abuses will instill a profound mistrust in a child but mistrust also develops just as powerfully with smaller, seemingly insignificant traumas. If we could watch a movie of our own conditioning and upbringing, we would probably be astounded at how many painful and difficult situations we went through. The traumas begin in the manner in which most of us are born and perhaps even earlier in utero if our mother was troubled or the home environment was stressful in some way. They continue in countless ways after that.

They occur in the pressures, expectations, fears, and frustrations of our parents. They occur in the roles that children are forced to play that violate their nature such as being a caretaker or the emotional support for a parent or being expected to follow in the footsteps of a parent's career or wished-for career. The most stringent expectations often come from frustrated parents who want to see their son or daughter do what they never could. In the poignant movie, *Shine*, David's father abuses his gifted son mercilessly because he himself was a frustrated musician and he genuinely feels that he is behaving in a supportive and loving way when he pressures his son to excel at the piano. The painful thing is that David loves playing the music but as it is mixed with his father's expectations it becomes too overwhelming for his nervous system and he never has a chance to feel what he really wants.

In our workshops, we often ask how many people were physically beaten as children and we are always amazed at the number of people who raise their hands. Physical abuse in the form of beatings or spankings is still considered routine. Given the life stresses that many parents suffer and the physical abuse that they probably experienced themselves as children, it is understandable that they would beat their children. But that does not minimize the abuse to the child. Furthermore, at its root, the child becomes simply an outlet for the parent's pent-up frustrations and repressions and through the beating the child comes to disrespect and hate him or herself.

On a more subtle level, traumas occur in the form of any physical or emotional abandonment that might seem trivial in retrospect but overwhelming to a defenseless child. Normally, we associate abandonment with physical separation such as when a parent leaves the household or is seldom at home. But we experience profound abandonment whenever we sense a lack of synchronicity with our mother or father such as not being listened to or understood or asked to play a role that goes against our nature. In short, we may have had many traumatic experiences as children that we may consider insignificant, routine, and ordinary but often we fail to recognize how powerfully they have destroyed our trust in ourselves and others.

Here are some examples from a recent workshop:

Lilly had a younger sister who was sick and she was told to be sweet and quiet so as not to disturb her. Now she is terrified of being angry and confronting anyone and she is constantly allowing herself to be invaded and disrespected, which makes it impossible for her to enter into deep relating.

Anders had a mother with asthma whom he had to take care of. He has become a heart surgeon who is unable to take time off from work to do what he loves to do. It feels like a deep threat to his existence not to be constantly working to help other people. The pressure to work and help is making him very unhappy, but he is trapped by his own fears of letting his mother down.

Lars had a violent father and an alcoholic mother and never felt that there was any space for his needs. The result today is that he listens to everyone and feels frustrated when nobody has the time for him.

Marit formed a "special" relationship as her father's pet but, in reality, she was his secret lover who replaced her mother whom he never loved. This created very confusing feelings of feeling special and at the same time not really having her father totally. She cannot have close relationships to women today because she still carries guilt toward her mother and feels alienated from her own sex. On top of this she has a constant pressure to look desirable and feels that her only sense of self is through being wanted by a man.

Alan was not wanted as a child and developed a deep shame for even existing. Today he frequently experiences deep depressions.

Jan was given a boy's name because her parents wanted a son not a daughter. She denied her femininity, hating everything female to please her parents and get their love, and in this process ended up hating and rejecting herself. It is now very difficult for her to receive a man, as she feels deeply humiliated for being a woman.

Trauma occurs commonly to a child whose parent or parents are too narcissistic to recognize or give meaningful attention to him or her. In fact, parental narcissism is probably one of the biggest sources of childhood trauma because it comes out in so many ways. Narcissistic parents often do not listen but lecture or give advice; they do not see or support the child's natural interests and gifts but push the child into avenues of their own preference. They mold the child according to their own morals or repress a child's natural energies because of fears of disapproval from others.

A close friend still suffers from the trauma of having a profoundly narcissistic mother. In his childhood, the attention she gave him was mostly a reflection of her own needs and whims. At a young age, he began to play the guitar and discovered that he had an unusual gift. He began practicing and even composing his own music. His father supported him to some extent but his mother was not even aware that he played until he gave concert years later at a local club. Her narcissism was so extreme that it even extended to sexual abuse. She would parade around the house with little clothing on to get his attention or ask him to give his appreciation while she tried on clothes that she had just bought. Over the years, he has had to work through profound confusion between his natural love for her as his mother and his absolute rage for how she treated him.

Our parents and the societies in which we were raised were not conscious enough to provide us with the loving, caring, sensitive, expansive, empowering support that we needed. Even if our parents meant well they may not have known better than to pass on the shame and guilt that they had received themselves. In the mind of a young, helpless, and vulnerable child, any kind of insensitivity is perceived as a deeply traumatic event. In time, the child's openness and sensitivity pull deeper and deeper inside to a place that is safe and untouchable. Even though we learn to cultivate an external personality that can relate and function (to some extent), the deeper layers of ourselves become hidden and removed. These deeper layers often do not get challenged until later when we enter into intimate love relationships or form significant relationships with authority figures. There we may suddenly realize that we are not open or that we are easily hurt.

A client of ours has suffered from migraine headaches. She noticed that she recently had a strong headache after visiting her parents and wondered if there was any connection. During the visit, her father saw that she was reading a book by John Bradshaw on shame. He took the book, hit her over the head with it, teased her about needing to read such a book, and suggested that perhaps she no longer needed to "indulge her feelings so much." She told us that her mother also suffered from migraines and was wondering if there might be some genetic connection. We suggested to her that although there might be some physical propensity for the women in her family to get migraines, it seems much more likely that the male chauvinistic, shaming, and humiliating behavior of her father toward her and her mother and toward women in general is the cause of the migraines. The only way the sensitivity can respond to that kind of aggression is by pulling in and creating pain in the body. The pain is like a small child inside calling out for attention.

After several years of doing growth workshops, first in America and then in India, I (Krish) returned to the United States and went to visit my parents. In the past, I had mostly idealized them. I remember quite vividly in one of the workshops in India, one of the therapists said to me, "If your childhood was so wonderful, then why are you so shut down emotionally, so in your head and controlled." I knew she had a point but I could not connect with the reason I was like that. Also, I felt torn inside. My family life had seemed very loving and supportive and I sincerely felt that my parents were both caring and kind people (still do). I did not want to blame them. At the same time, I wanted to go deeper into myself and into my emotions and that meant seeing and feeling things from the perspective of a traumatized child. This time, when I went home, I experienced things very differently. I could see what it had been like to grow up in my family.

I noticed my father's repressed anger and my mother's way of controlling others and her environment by giving advice and not listening. I had not really focused on these aspects of my parent's personalities before. Now I could see how frightening it must have been for me as a child. I also noticed that the way they related to each other and to others was superficial, polite, and false. Furthermore, the speed, the rationality, and the values of performance, prestige, and achievement that ran the family environment were painful to watch. I could see that all of this must have been deeply shocking to any sensitive child whose essence is "being" and not "doing." I coped well by joining the party and becoming polite, conformist, and a super-doer, but my sensitivity and my rebellion became buried under the pressure to become. The pressure and the values of achievement became my values, and my vulnerability and individuality were buried under all of it.

Later, when I started to read about recovering from codependency, it helped me to penetrate even more deeply behind my denial. For instance, reading in Robert Subby's great little book, *Lost in the Shuffle,* about the unspoken rules that govern dysfunctional families, I could see how my own family was dominated by these rules. Most of those he mentions such as not talking about any problems, not showing emotions, having unrealistic expectations placed on the child, putting others' needs above your own, not rocking the boat, not talking about sex, not being irresponsible or playful, and not learning to trust oneself—all of these totally dominated my family conditioning. These rules cause us to develop deep shame and fear inside and to lose touch with our spontaneous aliveness and joy of life.

Connecting the Past with the Present

I (Amana) grew up in a family where showing feelings and talking about your problems was unthinkable. My father was the only one who ever showed feelings and only when drunk. Then he would either be angry and judgmental of someone else or he would be crying and not wanting to live any longer. My mother dealt with the situation by becoming very practical and hard and not showing anything on the outside. She never talked to anybody about the situation but kept it a secret even to her own parents or close friends. As a child I remember feeling the tensions in the house and feeling completely alienated. Whenever I was sad, I would lock myself into the bathroom so nobody could see me crying. One time I decided that I was never going to show anybody what I really felt.

I could see in my mother's face the fear and disturbance whenever I was sad, angry, or frightened by something, and the criticism was always: "You are just like your father"—meaning irresponsible, weak, a loser, not satisfied with anything, complaining, and so on. I closed myself inside to the point where I became very numb. It took me a long time to finally be able to feel and show my feelings and not feel ashamed for feeling them. And it has taken me even longer to overcome the impending doom of my father's depression and destructiveness, which has been like a shadow and threat whenever I go through a difficult time. I still have tremendous difficulties reaching out for help and this is something I am slowly learning.

Some years ago I had an operation on my foot and experienced for the first time since very early childhood what it was like to be utterly helpless. It brought up a deep panic of not getting my needs met and a tremendous shame for having to ask for anything and not being able to take care of myself. It is ingrained in my system to take care of myself and unthinkable to ask for help or be dependent on someone. I was hypersensitive and angry when Krish wasn't as tuned into my needs as I would have liked and felt ashamed when I had to ask him frequently whenever I needed something.

It touched feelings of humiliation that I can see are linked directly to my mother, who unconsciously resented taking care of me and having to stay at home, while my father was out partying. Until this operation I had always assumed that my difficulty in asking for anything and needing from somebody had to do with the fact that my father was so needy and emotional and took all the space. His needs were always more important and the threat of his leaving to go on another drinking tour was always in the air. We had to adjust and I became so good at adjusting that I lost touch with my own feelings and needs.

Now I see that this is only part of the story. Although I have no clear recollection of ever being shamed for my needs, my mother became pregnant with me when she was only eighteen years old. She wanted to get away from her highly controlling parents and recognized that getting married and having a child was her escape. Since my father did not change his life in any way after I was born, my mother was left to carry the full responsibility of having a child. Her caring for me was mixed with resentment. She was overjoyed to have a child and she sincerely loved children, but still she resented that she couldn't go out with friends as frequently and had to stay home to nurse me. Because of my father's utter lack of responsibility and my mother's unspoken resentment,

I adapted very early by becoming self-sufficient. It wasn't safe to need anything and it was terrifying to be dependent.

> *We want to stress that recognizing the connection between present mistrust and fear and past traumas does not mean that we have to cast blame on anyone. The vast majority of parents and teachers do the very best they can in raising and teaching children. But we are all limited by our areas of unconsciousness and by the heritage that we import from our conditioning.*

Paying Attention to Our Emotional Reactions Moment to Moment

It is frightening to take away our veils because when we shatter our illusions, we also realize that the support and love that we may have imagined we received was not what it seemed. But as we become more aware of how strongly our past influences our present, it is much easier to observe our reactions moment to moment in our life today. Our emotions get easily triggered because we have so much residual from our past. But we have observed something quite miraculous in ourselves and in those we work with.

> *By simply watching and accepting our emotions, we transform.*

With increasing awareness, the emotional pull to react becomes less compelling. By watching with a loving and understanding heart, we gradually come out of the robotic behavior or out of the reactive child who is unobserved and out of control. We develop choice. This process soothes our soul and heals our wounds. In this process of paying attention to our emotional reactions and feelings moment to moment, we naturally begin to drop our resentments and appreciate and feel gratitude for those who raised us. We can see them for who they are or were and appreciate whatever they gave us.

Exercise:

Reflect on some of the invasion and abandonment traumas you experienced as a child.

Ask yourself:

1. *How must this experience have felt to a small child?*

2. *What kind of lasting effect would this kind of experience have had for this child?*

3. *How does this affect my relationships today?*

* * *

CHAPTER 4:

WHEN THE REGRESSED CHILD TAKES OVER –

Learning to Watch How We Act Out

A reaction is automatic; it is built in.
Somebody smiles, you smile.
Somebody is angry, you become angry.
The other creates you, you simply react.
A response is conscious.
The other may be angry,
but you decide whether to be angry or not.
Osho

We had a woman in a workshop recently in Italy who was very insistent on being able to speak whenever we had an open sharing. Because there were twenty-four other people in the room who also wanted time to share, it became a problem for us as well as for her. When we passed over her even though she was one of the first to raise her hand, she became very angry and disturbed. We told her that at times, she would have to contain her frustration and feel whatever this brought up for her, and that this containment was an important part of the work. Slowly, she was able to find more space inside to hold her frustration and she recognized the part of her that thought it would die if it didn't get the attention at the moment that she wanted it. When she remained with the feelings of frustration, gradually something began to relax and she gained insight that the panic and desperation was not all of her even though, when it took over, it felt that way. She discovered that she had the strength not to get what she wanted and still be OK.

How often, in a moment of feeling insulted, injured, or humiliated, do we react emotionally and irrationally and then harbor resentment for ages? Or perhaps, we may not even register the insult in the moment it occurs because we are in shock. Then we feel deeply resentful and abused afterward and ruminate incessantly about the things we should have said or would like to have said. We have harbored rancor inside for all the times in our life that we felt invaded or betrayed and were unable to express the hurt and anger that we felt. The hurt becomes buried inside and gets stuck in the body waiting to be provoked.

Getting to Know Our Regressed Child

Most of us can recognize a part inside that is full of panic, hungry for attention, and can be extremely entitled, reactive, and emotional, especially when things don't go our way. It is an inner space that behaves and thinks like a child but is housed in the body of an adult. That's why it's called *"a regressed child."* It is important for us to get to know this part—how it thinks, feels, and behaves because there are many times when this part takes over and, at best, all we can do is watch. It doesn't want to grow up. It is much like an unconscious force that comes out strongly and unpredictably regardless of what our "adult" personality would like. It lives perpetually in either fantasy trust or global mistrust. It can't stand being deprived and it wants what it wants now! Try telling a child who wants an ice cream cone to wait until tomorrow. Tomorrow doesn't exist for the child. Our regressed child inside is just the same way.

For instance, Cynthia is on a special diet and chooses to eat a smoothie for lunch and skip breakfast. Adam, her boyfriend loves to cook and spend long leisurely lunches together with Cynthia. He gets angry and moody when she has her smoothie because he misses their time together and often makes derisive comments about her diet and her weight. Cynthia feels anxious when he gets moody or pulls away and loses heart when he comments on her efforts to eat healthily and lose weight. So she often gives up her regime to join him for lunch but later feels angry with herself and resentful with Adam. Both of them are highly successful in their lives and in most areas except their interpersonal relationships, behave rationally, responsibly and predictably.

Rolando and Alicia have been a couple for five years. He has been very attached to their passionate sexuality but lately, he has been feeling less turned on to her. He finds that he avoids making love, feels attracted to other women, and often flirts with them. When questioned about what might be influencing the change, he claims that he is finding defects in her physical appearance as she gets older, especially more wrinkles, and she seems less passionate in their sexuality. He also says that sometimes for no apparent reason, he gets angry and abrasive with her.

In both of these examples, the problem is the same. Rolando, Adam, and Cynthia are being taken over by their regressed child. Adam and Cynthia lack the awareness and tools to deal with the fact that each person has different needs, and Rolando is not accepting the fact that deepening relating brings predictable changes in sexuality.

When we are in our regressed child we feel, think, and behave like any child would. We don't like to defer gratification, and do not want to contain the frustration when we are not getting what we want. More deeply, we do not want to feel the pain or the fear when we are being disrespected or are not getting our immediate needs met. Typically, our regressed child is reactive, emotional, impatient, controlling, manipulative, dishonest, political, irresponsible, blaming, analyzing, righteous, impetuous, aggressive, collapsed, easily prone to addictions, and full of conscious or unconscious expectations of others and life. This kind of behavior is guaranteed to create problems in all aspects of our life.

Our regressed child does not live in the present. It is not forming conclusions based on the reality today nor is it responding appropriately to current situations. Its beliefs and behavior are conditioned by past traumatic experiences, many of which are unconscious. It is our regressed child that holds on to resentments from a perceived or real disrespect or sinks into resignation or despair after a rejection, loss or disappointment. No matter how on top of things or mature we imagine ourselves to be, there will be times when we get triggered. We may try to rigidly structure our lives to minimize disturbances, but it doesn't work; life has a way of disturbing our "tranquility."

> *These disturbances are valuable experiences because they are the ways that we connect with our regressed child and discover how much our consciousness is affected by the past, and how little trust of others and self we actually have.*

We will describe in general terms what this part of us is like. But the details and fine-tuning of getting to know this part depends on each one of us finding the willingness and making the effort to look at ourselves closely and honestly.

Our Regressed Child is Transmitting Messages All the Time

Whether we are aware of it or not, our regressed child is transmitting its fears, insecurities, needs, wants, and expectations all the time. We call this, "radio codependency." These unconscious messages cause people to react to us in ways that confirm our fears and deepen our mistrust. These messages are directed toward other people such as "I would like you to take care of me." "I am not going to let you in." "I want you to make me feel OK about myself." "Give me all your attention." Even though usually unspoken and unconscious, the other person feels the vibration as if we are transmitting a signal. That's why we call it, "radio codependency." The main problem is not the message itself but that it is unconscious and that it pushes people away without our knowing the reason. Often our words contradict the messages we are sending out energetically, and so we don't understand why people react to us the way they do. We feel rejected or let down and this mechanism reinforces our mistrust of others.

Sometimes, someone in a workshop will say that he or she wants a lover or friend to accept the person the way he or she is. But often, our regressed child is demanding, manipulative, vengeful, impatient, and cruel. Nobody needs to accept that kind of behavior especially if we ourselves are not willing to take some responsibility to see and understand this part of us.

> *Until we become conscious and can take responsibility for ourselves, we often need, at the moment when we "act out" from our regressed child, for someone to set firm yet loving limits on this behavior. This can become a way that we eventually learn to set that limit ourselves to our regressed child inside, when he or she is acting out. Just like a loving parent would set loving limits when a child is acting out.*

It takes quite some willingness to look at ourselves honestly and to understand this young and wounded part that is full of fear and shame; it is operating under our consciousness. We have learned to survive the best way we could and we still believe that these survival strategies are necessary. Paradoxically, the more we understand this part of us and the more we can embrace it with love and compassion, the less we are taken over by it. It is also helpful, when we notice this part of us coming up, to take the time to feel our underlying discontent and perhaps identify its origin.

Recently we were doing a workshop at a seminar center. A woman who lives and works there was preparing food for the group. She was not happy and was fully in the grips of her regressed child. Whenever we would come a few minutes late for a meal because we were finishing a process, she would make some nasty comment to one of our assistants. Even when we told her one time with much advanced notice that we would be coming late, her only response was, "OK, then everyone will just have to eat cold food." We have both known this person for a long time and know that she behaves like this when she feels stressed or unhappy.

She had been working and living at this center for years and it was no longer right for her. She was clinging to the security of living there and this was making her bitchy and miserable. Eventually she recognized that she was acting out and was unhappy with her life situation and began to confront the underlying cause. Later that year, she took the risk to make a change, moving out on her own and finding other work. When we saw her a year later, she was enjoying her life.

Symptoms of the Regressed Child

It is not easy to see when our regressed child has taken over because often we have been operating from that space for so long that we actually think it is who we are. We have no means of comparison. But we can begin to tell by understanding and recognizing some of the most common symptoms.

1. Moodiness and Tantrums

Our regressed child has little ability to tolerate frustration. We are holding a great deal of unconscious fear and anxiety inside. Some of the time, we are able to contain that anxiety but when we don't get what we want or when life's circumstances are not nurturing, we can easily become unglued. The tension of holding everything together and the anger that arises when life and others don't support us shows itself in moods and tantrums. The tension starts to leak out and is fueled by a righteous anger that we should not have to feel this discomfort.

Depending on our emotional nature, the manner in which our regressed child reacts and behaves differs. Some of us react outwardly—we may throw a tantrum, get angry, storm out of a room, or outwardly try to punish the person who provokes us. Others withdraw and express the hurt and anger by withholding the energy from the person who hurt us. Or we may have become so accustomed to being disappointed that we are in a deep state of resignation. We may live together with someone but we may have stopped communicating our feelings and live in a deep emotional isolation. All of these styles are different forms of acting out.

Of all the forms of reaction, the two that seem deepest for me (Krish) are irritation and withdrawal. When I am anxious, disturbed, or hurt, I first get irritated or angry, and then I pull inside where no one can touch me or hurt me again. Often, I don't even know that I am disturbed or hurt but I can feel myself getting moody or irritable. I have explored this deeply and discovered that the source of this behavior is deep inner stress to perform and feeling unseen and unacknowledged. The two forces operating inside are a constant drive to perform and mistrust that I will ever be recognized and appreciated. In this kind of inner stress and pain, I deny my emotional needs and feelings.

I (Amana) have a very similar way of reacting to hurts. I may get angry later, but my first reaction is to pull inside, withdraw, and pull away energetically and physically from the person who hurt me. I learned early that it wasn't safe to show my feelings so I simply took all the energy inside and allowed myself to be sad only when I was alone. Because my father behaved like a child—highly emotional and irresponsible—I had to be there for him and his feelings and there was no space for mine. So being together with Krish, who has the same emotional reaction to pull inside when he gets hurt, it is a continual challenge for both of us to take a step out of resignation, to have the courage to connect and to share what is really happening instead of staying in a state of withdrawal, isolation, and resignation.

2. Irresponsible Behavior

Our regressed child is in action when we engage in irresponsible behavior such as arriving late or not at all to appointments, borrowing things and not returning them, leaving messes for others to clean up, not taking care of basic practical matters in life. It is usually a dysfunctional way of expressing an unconscious desire to be taken care of. Or it may be a way of expressing that we are unhappy with how we are living our lives and the child inside is acting out and frustrated.

Some friends of ours have a relating dynamic that illustrates this very clearly. She likes the house to be neat. He, on the other hand, could not care less about how tidy things are. He leaves messes everywhere. She feels betrayed when she feels that she has to clean up after him, like a mother having to clean up after a child, and she starts to feel like an angry raging bitch, which reminds her of how her mother was with her father. She feels and believes that to get love from a man, she has to take care of his needs but when he starts to take this for granted, she feels betrayed. Meanwhile, he can't see that by leaving little messes around, he is behaving like a regressed child expecting his mother to clean up after him. All he sees is an angry bitch raging at him. When this happens, both of them feel betrayed and both are in their mistrust wounds.

3. Spacing Out, Collapse, Illness, or Depression

Sometimes we feel overwhelmed by life. At those times, our behavior can easily be taken over by our regressed child who wants to find some way of hiding from challenge and responsibility.

We may space out, become sick, become depressed, or simply find ourselves with no energy. When this happens, it is helpful to recognize that the child inside feels overwhelmed, may be overcome with fear; remember to be loving toward ourselves. Of course, not all illness or depression is an unconscious acting out of our regressed child, but many times, it is.

I (Krish) recognize that whenever I come to a new environment, especially a big city, (which we do often in our work) I feel overwhelmed and I regress. I will watch TV or just space out and sometimes Amana can be asking me a question and I simply don't hear her. At those times, I find it a struggle to do the most mundane things of life. Recognizing my regression and taking time to feel the fear, I usually recover quite quickly.

I (Amana) have tremendous fear of expressing my creativity and exposing myself. I was brought up in Denmark, a very small country, where the value is to fit in, to adapt, and become invisible. So when I started putting myself out in the workshops, I had to face immense fear and shame. The voices inside were saying: "You don't have anything to give," "Who do you think you are" and so on. Because of this continual attack inside, my regressed child would sometimes take over and give up.

The pressure was simply too much and I would get sick or be so tired I could hardly move. It has taken a lot for me to be able to love and listen to the feelings of this regressed child and give her the time and space she needs to deal with the situation. I went through a process of taking her by the hand and holding her when she would get very scared of the exposure and receiving the energy of so many people. Slowly it became easier and easier and now during our workshops the shaming voices inside are far away or gone and I seldom hear them.

4. Self-Sabotaging Behavior

Sometimes our regressed child expresses itself in some indirect way because without knowing it, we are terrified or unhappy. For instance, we may be doing something important but are so afraid of failing or even succeeding, that we sabotage ourselves. Other times, we are in a situation where we are unhappy but we are unaware of it and express the unhappiness in our actions.

During medical school, I (Krish) had a hard time because my heart was not really into being a doctor. At that time, I did not know that my calling was to move into psychiatry and work with people's emotional and spiritual growth not with their physical problems. In my conditioning, emotional problems were considered a bit of an indulgence and the "real" issues were physical. I acted out by sometimes slacking off on scut work (the menial chores of a medical student such as drawing blood, running down lab results, and so on) and not being totally responsible in my care of patients.

Once, I left the hospital before I had taken care of all the small details for a patient and made sure she was fully taken care of because I wanted to go home and jog before it got dark. The next morning, I caught hell from my senior resident. He was perfectly right and I felt horribly guilty. It was only later when I did my residency in psychiatry, that I understood why I had behaved that way. When we love what we do, it is natural for us to be total, efficient, mindful, and caring in our work. I loved every aspect of my psychiatry residency and it showed in my work.

5. Craving Attention, Not Listening or Being Insensitive to Others, and Exaggerating Our Accomplishments

We have an old acquaintance who is difficult to be with because when we are together, he obsessively talks about himself and is not particularly interested in listening to others. Many of us can identify a similar tendency—it is merely a cover for profound shame and insecurity. From this insecure inner space, we may brag about our accomplishments, exaggerate things we have done to impress people, even lie just to make ourselves seem bigger than we feel inside.

This kind of grandiosity is just a flip side of feeling deficient and wanting approval and respect from someone we admire. In this case, just by being close to someone we esteem, we hope we will get the self-respect we are lacking. When we are with someone whom we hold as an authority figure, this desperate need for recognition, approval or validation can drive us to say and do things that may be humiliating but we can't seem to help ourselves.

6. Rescuing and Advising

One of the more subtle ways that our regressed child acts out is in a role of the rescuer and advice giver. This can be deceptive because it appears to be adult and well-meaning behavior but under the surface, there can be a regressed child who wants to be in control, feel needed or feel useful. The motivation and the energy behind it, rather than the behavior itself, defines it as a regressed child. If we are rescuing or advising as a power game, to get a need met, then it is simply our regressed child in disguise. If we are compulsive in this behavior, or using it to avoid our own feelings of insecurity and fear, then it is the regressed child in action.

7. The Regressed Child in Sex

When the regressed child takes over in our sex life, it can be trouble. Normally we are not aware of how this happens. There is a phenomenon that we call "the hungry penis" or "the hungry vagina." Our desperate need for approval, recognition, filling up and relief of anxiety, rather than being acknowledged, accepted, and felt, gets acted out in sex. When the other person feels that we want sex not to make love but to fill a need inside, he or she can easily feel repelled and not interested. But since this is rarely conscious and dealt with, it can cause the sexuality and the relationship to suffer.

And there is more. There is also "the angry penis" or the angry vagina." In this case, anger, rather than needs, becomes expressed indirectly. Many of us have stored up anger, even rage, at the opposite sex that we may not be in touch with. Because sex is such a powerful energy, it can surface while making love. Then our lovemaking can become a catharsis rather than an intimacy. It is good if such feelings are surfacing because once conscious, they can be dealt with. But, in our experience, lovemaking is not the appropriate place to play out our rage.

A client was sharing recently with me (Krish) that he gets angry when his wife rejects him sexually. His reaction has been to either get moody or demanding. "In the past," he went on to say, "if I demanded enough, I could get my way. But that doesn't work anymore since she started therapy and doing workshops. Don't you think," he asked, "that since she is my wife, she should be available to make love when I want to?" (He had some work to do!)

8. *"Godzilla Meets Frankenstein"*

We bring to our relationships a history of being invaded, betrayed, and hurt and this history creates a reoccurring pattern of regressed behavior. All too often, one person's pattern fits directly into the other's so that each one triggers the other's wound. In our work, we call this "Godzilla meets Frankenstein"—two regressed mistrusting children, each in his or her own movie, squaring off in the boxing ring where each person's wound has been triggered and each feels deeply misunderstood and unloved. In this kind of situation, neither person can hear or understand the other because both are lost in a regressed trance of mistrust coming from a primal wound.

A couple who are close friends of ours were telling us recently of a scene that they go through repeatedly. When they go to a party, she feels very insecure because she is convinced that he is having all the fun, getting all the attention and even flirting with other women. He is enjoying socializing with other people including other women and does not want to be controlled. The situation is a setup for each of their deepest wounds to be triggered—hers of feeling abandoned, his of feeling controlled.

As the evening goes on, she becomes more and more jealous and more and more miserable. Eventually, she asks to leave. He is having a great time and doesn't want to leave when she does. When they finally get in the car together to go home, she has a fit—blaming him for being so rejecting, for giving attention to other women and for being all together such an utter "shithead." He feels manipulated, misunderstood, and invaded since, as he sees it, he was just having a good time and not doing anything to hurt her and he is resentful that he gave in to leave.

The woman in this couple is having her own particular nightmare re-enacted. Her father (a psychiatrist) was never available for her and she felt that she had to beg for his attention. The man in the couple had a mother who was overbearing and possessive and he mistrusts women because he feels he has to constantly protect his freedom from invasion.

From the perspective of their regressed child, they are perfectly right. She feels deprived and he feels invaded. But with closer introspection, they can also see how the present situation is a re-enactment and their being together allows them to access, feel, and heal their wounds. From our own experience in relationship and working with countless couples, it is obvious to us that with the people that matter most in our life, we will always create situations that provoke our deepest mistrust and by doing so have the opportunity to heal and feel what we couldn't in the past.

9. Addictive Behavior

One of the most profound ways that our regressed child shows itself is in addictive behavior. We define addictive behavior as anything we do in order not to feel our fear or pain. Most of us have some way that we do this. It can be by using substances (such as alcohol, mood-altering drugs, food, nicotine, or caffeine). The addictive behavior can be television or movie watching, shopping, or continuously staying busy. It can be with routines—ways that we structure our life in such a way that we become robotic and unconscious. It can be by isolating ourselves or by compulsive socializing.

My father (Krish) was a highly sensitive and introverted man who relied strongly on habits and routines to nourish himself. After he retired, he became an accomplished musician and he would spend much of his day practicing the bassoon. He planned every day of his life with a series of routines and would move from one to the other (reading, playing tennis, practicing, and listening to music) as the day went on, often quite oblivious to people around him. It worked well for him but it was also a cover for his extreme difficulty expressing his feelings and sharing himself with others, even those closest to him. I learned much the same style. It wasn't until I realized that all these habits and routines were blocking my own ability to come close to someone that something changed for me. Substance abuse was never attractive to me because I have the strong inner discipline that I learned from my father. But just like him, habits and routines became my addictive behavior. It is a deep expression of shyness and mistrust. Now, I can see more clearly when I use these habits to escape from relating, especially with Amana. I can feel the distance they create and it hurts.

Addictive behavior is an attempt of our regressed child to nurture him or herself. But mixed with our shame and our shock, it can also carry a big flavor of self-destructiveness. We are trying in some way to fill the emptiness inside but at the same time, when we see ourselves doing something harmful to our bodies or compulsively distracting ourselves from our emotional and spiritual growth, we hate ourselves for it. It takes much understanding and self-compassion to penetrate addictive behavior and replace it with nourishing and healthy activities.

Observing with Love and Understanding

When we bring love and understanding to our regressed child with all his or her behaviors, the panic starts to recede and our reactions occur less frequently. A space grows inside that is vast enough to contain the feelings of this wounded part of us, and we do not necessarily need to act on those feelings. This process takes time, but grows steadily when we do not repress or spiritualize our fears away.

As we watch with a deep willingness to know ourselves, our consciousness grows. Then there is not just a child acting out, repeatedly re-creating distancing and mistrust scenes and indulging in blame. We can begin to identify our patterns and recognize the type of situations and people that trigger our regressed child. We can recognize when the regressed child has taken over. He or she has a definite inner feeling and we can learn to identify that feeling when it comes up.

Sometimes we can choose not to act out and sometimes we can't. The real art, in our experience, is to watch ourselves and accept what we see without wanting to be where we are not or thinking that we should be different. This takes courage because it is painful to see and feel our strong reactions and moodiness. It is also painful to feel discontent and to receive the rejections and disapproval that behaving like a child provokes.

When we are compassionate and understanding with ourselves, slowly more space is created and when we can allow ourselves to truly feel the pain and fear that is provoked inside, the energy shifts and maturity starts happening.

We are not suggesting to indulge our regressed feelings and behavior—but rather to strike a delicate balance that does not include either repression or overindulgence. What we are suggesting is simply a willingness to identify, understand, and explore the roots of this part of us. We end with a small example from our own lives. Recently, Amana needed to have an operation on her foot because of an accident that happened while hiking in Bali. For weeks after the operation, she was in pain and quite incapacitated.

I needed to take care of her and to manage all the practical details around the house. I never realized how many practical things there are to do until I was forced to do all of them (a common male trait, I suspect). Also, I began to notice that I was getting disturbed by all that I had to do and the helplessness of being unable to take her pain away. To make matters worse, in the middle of this, we had to do a three-day workshop. I judged myself for not being a more compassionate and caring nurse (I think that on the whole, doctors make poor nurses).

Then I recalled that when I was a seven-year-old child, my mother was hospitalized for a year with a serious case of TB and I was left in the care of a maid and my father who was working most of the time. I had repressed the abandonment feelings of this episode occurring at such a vulnerable time in my life. Recalling this buried memory helped me to understand why this situation with Amana's injury was provoking my regressed child so strongly. All of a sudden, Amana was not available as she had been before—normally so caring, proficient, and attentive to me and to the many details of everyday living.

When we regress, we may not have the option to prevent our acting out. But we always have the option to learn from the experience.

Exercise:

Recall recently when you found yourself reacting with anger or pulling away.

Ask yourself:

1. *What was triggering me?*

2. *Why did I get angry or pull away? Why was I upset?*

3. *What was the fear or hurt that I was feeling at that time?*

4. *What was the need that was not being met?*

* * *

PART 2:

BREAKING OUT
OF FANTASY TRUST

CHAPTER 5:

"THE BOX" –

The Prison of Our Conditioning

For millions of years,
our whole way of life has been of adjustment, of compromise.
And compromise with whom?
with the crowd – with which everybody else is also compromising,
where nobody is opening up his reality,
where everyone is afraid of being himself
because from the very beginning he has been told,
"The way you are is not going to be acceptable."
Osho

W e have found that no matter how much inner work we do on ourselves, unless we take the step of separating from our conditioning, we cannot learn to trust ourselves—or another person either.

By separating, we mean a process of learning to experience ourselves in a way that is not programmed by our past conditioning.

This process takes tremendous courage. In order to understand the significance of separating, we start by discussing the power of conditioning—what we call "the box."

I (Krish) remember one poignant moment when I was in my last year in high school. A student in my class was brilliant but he never did any work and kept to himself most of the time. After school, he would hang out by himself in a little cafe around the corner from the school. I always considered him an interesting fellow but tended to avoid him because I thought he was a bit strange and I was too busy working hard to be at the top of the class and trying to be one of the best athletes in the school. One day, I was walking home from school and I happened to pass by the cafe. I decided to go in and chat with him. I sat down at his table. For a while, he was silent and then out of the blue, he said,

"Hey, Trobe, don't you realize that it's all bullshit?"

"What's all bullshit?" I asked

"All this stuff that you're doing all the time. Trying to be the best all the time, kissing the ass of all the teachers. Your whole trip is bullshit, don't you see? Who the fuck are you doing all this for?"

"For me. I want to get into a good college."

"Man, don't you see that you are just a robot? Jesus! You're a smart guy, wise up and stop playing the stupid game."

At the time, I did not have a clue what he was talking about. I lost track of him after we graduated but I never forgot that conversation. I suspect that he probably had to go through his own emotional turmoil but years later, I realized that he knew something that I would not even begin to discover until after I had graduated from college.

Most of us have lost touch with ourselves. We have lost respect for ourselves and we are living life as others want or wanted us to live. And when we lose touch with ourselves, we stop trusting our own intelligence.

"The Box"

As children, we desperately need direction and guidance. We need to make some sense out of the world that we are discovering and some way of determining what is right and wrong. To a greater or lesser extent, our parents and, in a broader sense, the culture in which we are raised, gives us a code of behavior and a morality to live by. In so doing, our parents, and others who are important in our upbringing, give us what they sincerely believe a child needs in order to become a good and happy person.

However, there is a problem. First, if we never examine and question the guidance, rules, and morals we are given, they never truly become our own. We follow something somebody told us to do or be, without living out of our own understanding and intelligence. Secondly, the direction we are given is often strongly based on fear, repression and unconscious convention. And thirdly, those rules and ways of living may be totally appropriate for our parents and teachers but may not be the right thing for us. As a child, we do not have the consciousness or the resources to question the rules or the values we are given, we simply accept them unconsciously and become adapted without realizing what we have done. Many of us may grow up believing in the truth of what we have been given without questioning the values or morals and without seeing the limitation this brings to our lives.

We all have an inner voice that tells us what is right for us and how we want and need to live. And if we are encouraged to listen to this voice, we develop the intelligence to live accordingly. But for most of us, that inner voice has become difficult to hear because we were conditioned not to listen to it. We were taught to listen to "those who knew what was best for us." A child who is not supported to trust his or her own feelings and perceptions loses valuable self-respect and empowerment and develops insecurity and shame. Instead of being taught to develop our own intelligence, we are given a morality. Most parents believe that if they don't give their children a morality, they will turn out bad. But a child who is loved, supported and encouraged to develop his or her own values based on his or her own intrinsic intelligence will become a healthier, stronger, and more compassionate human being.

We call the code of conduct, standards, and values we are given as a child "the box." Figuratively speaking, we are each given a box and told, nonverbally or verbally, that if we live inside our box—think and behave in a certain way—then we will get love, respect, and approval. With the box, come certain rules and values that define what it means to be a good person and what will give us love, success, and respect. It is as though we are sitting inside our box and the rules, standards and morals that we are told to live by are written on the walls of the box.

Having these rules, standards, and moral code to refer to is, in a way, comforting. It gives us security and the knowledge that if we live according to the rules, we are "OK." Furthermore, the box also gives us an identity, a sense for who we are in this world, what role to play and how to be. As a child, I (Krish) lived quite comfortably in my box and I never suspected that it was limited in any way. I was so comfortable. I was taught that parents know what is best and that it is best to listen and follow their guidance. Often when our box is cozy, it takes us longer to break out. Unfortunately, it had little to do with who I was in my essence or what I needed for support to find myself.

My (Amana) process was different. Partly because I never had a consistent father, there was less comfort in my box, and I had an easier time seeing the lie of it.

There are some powerful movies, *Pleasantville* and *The Truman Show* that wonderfully show this whole process of growing up in a box and being given a false but conforming identity. We often show these movies in our workshops. Something may feel deeply wrong or empty to us inside but we may not know what it is because we have not ventured out of the box. The box is all we know. Being placed in this box is a profound betrayal of our essence and of our being, and limits our potential and our flowering. Inside the box true fulfillment is not possible.

The Conflict between the Desire for Truth and the Fear of Change

A strong mechanism keeps us from stepping out of the box or even becoming aware that we are in one. If we move away from the rules and conventions we have been given, we may very likely suffer a powerful attack of anxiety, fear, and guilt. These feelings are seldom rational. They come from primal fears of being exiled from those we love and from those we need for our survival.

Recently, we were doing a workshop in Japan and we had spent the afternoon doing strong and energetic exercises to support the participants to step out of the box. A woman was sharing her terrors of questioning the rules and of losing the support of her family and friends. We asked her what it means to be a friend. She said that to her a friend is someone you spend time with. She had not yet considered that if some of the people she spent time with were not supporting her flowering as a unique and self-loving person, perhaps they were not really her friends.

It is dangerous to do inner work because it awakens our intelligence and we begin to discover that many of the rules we have unconsciously accepted and lived by may no longer serve us. We discover that many of the things we were doing automatically no longer attracts us. That realization can be terrifying because it means that we need to make some radical changes in our life. We become torn between the passion for truth and the terror of change.

We encounter this conflict all the time in our work. Someone may come to a workshop and begin to question the values of his or her box, but when the person returns home and once again feels the pressures of the conventions and the people that he or she has been living with, it is too terrifying to continue to do inner work. Many people will book a workshop but cancel because of "sickness" or "family obligations" at the last moment. Often, one member of a couple will begin to do inner work and question the box he or she was raised in but feels that to continue would threaten the relationship and stops. Or people see that to question the box would jeopardize their relationship with their parents and family and this seems too terrifying a step to take. These fears are totally understandable.

Many of us are dreadfully afraid to disturb the beliefs and values we have lived with. Yet once we have tasted a little of the sweetness of truth and freedom it stays with us forever and becomes something that haunts us. Once we have seen the limitations we are living with, it is hard to continue to live like a robot without feeling the pain of living this way and wasting precious time.

> *The pull toward truth is generally stronger than the opposite pull toward fear and security. But it is so close, we joke that truth often wins only by a photo finish.*

Perhaps the most terrifying step any of us will ever take in life is to begin to challenge the rules and morality of our box. And in our experience, it is a lengthy process to question our conditioning and replace it with intelligence. Living without prescribed rules is frightening. Often what happens is that we discard our original box, replace it with a new one, and follow the rules of this new one as mindlessly as we did the first one. But that may be a necessary step to find the courage to step out in the first place. Eventually, we gain enough self-confidence and self-trust to live by our own intelligence moment to moment. We become able to respond to a situation from the here and now and not from an idea of the past. We become able to live without a box.

Identifying Our Box

The first step out of the box is to become aware that we are in one. That moment can become the beginning of a long process of self-inquiry.

You can identify your own particular box by asking yourself some specific questions:

1. *What did I have to do and what am I still doing to get love and attention?*

2. *What was I taught about what makes a good person? What ideas do I have today about what makes a good person?*

3. *What role did I have to play or am still playing to feel good about myself or to get respect and approval?*

4. *What was allowed and what was not allowed—for instance, in areas of sexuality, expression of anger, creativity, joy, sadness, or other emotions? What feelings do I judge myself for today in my life?*

Recently, I (Krish) was doing a session with an Italian man who was highly intelligent and successful in his work. His difficulty was that he no longer felt sexually attracted to his wife and was having affairs. One affair in particular had become deep and significant for him and gradually, he was spending more and more time with her. When I asked him if he had told his wife about this, he was astonished even at the idea of exposing this secret. "It would hurt her too much," he told me. Slowly, he came to see that it was his fears of disturbing the "harmony" of the marriage and family that prevented him from being honest. He clearly was not ready to be honest nor was he able to comprehend the price he was paying for his dishonesty. But it was a good first step for him to realize that it was his own fear that was preventing him and not being in the illusion that he was protecting his wife.

In his childhood, his father had always had affairs and his mother lamented to my client, her only son, about it. Now he is living just as his father did, in dishonesty and feeling guilty about it, but not having the courage to break free. He is sacrificing his self-respect and dignity without which he cannot grow into loving himself and becoming a whole person. The fear and panic of being honest is too overwhelming and so he chooses to stay in his box of dishonesty with an identity of someone who is not proud of himself.

Doing the Rage and Grief Work

It often happens that as our fantasies begin to shatter and we begin to see the negative aspects of our conditioning, we go through a period where we feel rage for the ways we were repressed, shut down, and given a false morality. This rage wakes up our inner strength and helps us find our trust again. It is a healthy energy that can clean out years of compliance and compromise. This rage extends not only to our parents but to the whole society in which we were raised for the ways that it stifles and abuses a child's innocence and trust. It extends toward the repressive values and non-supportive ways of raising children that our parents may not have been able to question. In fact, that negative conditioning is so pervasive and powerful that we seldom question it until we suddenly realize that our life is dysfunctional.

When I (Krish) started my residency in psychiatry, I recognized that I was entering into a world where I would probably have to confront many conservative ideas about why people have emotional problems. I must admit that from the start I felt like an angry rebel with a point of view. But I found a kindred soul in the outgoing chief resident. Like me, she was also interested in therapy and not so impressed with the strictly biological approach. Shortly after we met, she gave me Alice Miller's book, *The Drama of the Gifted Child*. I read that book in one evening and then proceeded to consume everything else she had written.

My chief resident friend then directed me to the work of Heinz Kohut. It helped me to understand in a way that I never had before precisely how a child gets traumatized by "normal conditioning." To grossly oversimplify, he explains that when a child receives the kind of positive mirroring that he or she needs, the child develops a sense of self and authenticity and a sense of capability to realize his or her potential. Positive mirroring means that the child's true self and potential is reflected back to him or her. But if this potential and real self is not mirrored, the child's personality fragments and as a result, he or she develops shame and profound insecurity. The child compensates for this profound shame by creating a false self and becoming overly narcissistic and self-preoccupied. I was just as Kohut described—narcissistic and self-preoccupied. I was compensated on the outside and deeply insecure inside. I also recognized this development in the patients I was working with.

There has been a strong trend in psychiatry (and particularly in the program at the University of California where I was studying) away from therapy and the psychological causes of emotional disorders toward biological causes. This approach brought up my rebel. I could feel how Western society seemed so addicted to quick fixes. Emotional work is deep and takes time and this biological trend seemed to be advocating that if we just take a pill, our anxieties and fears will go away. Furthermore, I felt that it moved away from the real solution, which involved elevating the consciousness of the society and the way children were being raised. I also felt that it fed the misconception that biology rather than social conditioning, schooling, and the family environment were the source of problems.

I remember some poignant moments during my residency when I came up against this situation. I was working on the adolescent ward and treating a teenager who had been admitted for depression. I talked with this teenager every day and came to learn his story. He was a highly sensitive child who felt pressured by his father to perform in school and in athletics. It was all too much for him and he withdrew deeply inside. I was asked to present the case in a Grand Rounds for the Psychiatry Department. (Grand Rounds is a conference where a resident presents a case and then the senior doctors discuss it and decide on a course of treatment.)

After I had talked about what brought him in and how he was doing after two weeks as an inpatient, the discussion mostly revolved around biological markers and tests for depression, which don't actually tell much anyway. Almost nothing was said about the psychodynamic issues involved. Then, they all concluded that he should be placed on antidepressants and spent the rest of the time discussing which medication to use. I went ballistic. First, I felt that I was making some progress with him and second, I felt that putting him on medication was totally inappropriate. It felt like sanctioning the abuse and taking the focus away from treating the whole family where it belonged. When I strongly objected and voiced my point of view, the attending physicians thought I was out of line to even question their opinion.

Another time, while I was still on the adolescent service, we were having a conference about the kind of music that the kids were listening to—music that was full of anger, obscenities, and rebellion against convention. The senior doctors felt that it was destructive for them to listen to this music because it provoked their acting out and their violence. I could not have disagreed more. I felt that this music was an important catharsis for them and it was expressing not only their shadow sides but also the shadow sides of their parents. It was expressing the fury that they held inside for growing up with so much repression and control and for having to swallow so many rules and false morality. We had a good fight about that one too. I think the staff doctors were happy when I finally graduated. I admit that I was over-reactive but I felt so strongly, "Stop repressing the kids! That's why they are here in the first place."

Our rage is often just the doorway to a profound feeling of sadness and grief for the child who suffered so much. Often we are so detached from this pain that we can at best feel it in others, especially children. After many years of building armor around our wounded heart, it is not easy to let it drop and feel the hurt inside. For some of us, our shock is so great that it takes tremendous patience and acceptance to begin to connect with our wounded being and actually feel the pain. We may need to spend much time just experiencing the shock inside. Sometimes a movie, a story, or seeing a helpless animal or child suffering or abused can open the door to our own sorrow and that may be a great beginning. The pain we see outside is a mirror of our own and this kind of identification can start our own feeling and healing process.

The process of questioning our conditioning and examining the box we were raised in does not mean that we need to hold on to anger or resentment. But we need to wake up this anger to connect with the strength we lost. We need our strength to be able to live fully here and now and to protect ourselves from anything that doesn't feel right. This strength brings us, in time, to a point of feeling genuine gratitude and appreciation for everything we received from our parents or caretakers.

When we regain our strength, we automatically let go of any illusion that we are a victim of bad conditioning. Everyone gets "bad" conditioning in the sense that it is unenlightened. But when we begin to live by our own intelligence we cease to be an unconscious clone. Furthermore, when we question the values, standards, and rules we inherited, it does not mean we have to reject all of our conditioning. It only means we reject aspects that no longer serve us, those that do not correspond to our own wisdom and intelligence.

Exercise:

Think of something that you have always wanted to do but were too afraid to do.

Ask yourself:

1. **What am I afraid of?**

2. **What might be the consequences of such an action?**

3. **What might be the benefits?**

* * *

CHAPTER 6:

THE CAMEL, THE LION, AND THE CHILD –

Friedrich Nietzsche's Developmental Stages

We can use the metaphors of Friedrich Nietzsche.
He says that man's life can be divided into
three successive metamorphoses of the spirit.
The first he calls "the camel,"
the second he calls, "the lion,"
and the third he call "the child."
Every human being has to draw upon and
assimilate the cultural heritage of his society.
You have to assimilate the whole past.
This is what Nietzsche calls "the camel stage."
But the time comes when the camel has to become a lion.
The lion proceeds to tear apart the
huge monster known as "thou shalt not."
It is good to become a lion
but one has still to take one more jump –
and that jump is to become the child.
The first childhood is a false childhood,

the second childhood is the real childhood.
The second childhood is called the "stage of the sage."
Osho

Edward booked a workshop with us, never having done any emotional work on himself before. He had no idea what he was getting into, he wasn't even sure why he was there and called twice to cancel but kept changing his mind and in the end showed up. A friend had referred him because, she told him, that his relationship life was a mess and he needed help. Edward is a highly successful lawyer, dresses fashionably, and he lives the jet-set life-style—eating at expensive restaurants, having two elaborate apartments in different cities, driving a fancy car, going on ski holidays at the best resorts in Europe, and having had a long history of short-term relationships with models and aspiring movie stars.

In the beginning of the workshop, Edward was very resistant. When we were talking about all of us carrying wounds from our childhood and covering up our fears and insecurities with compensations, he could not understand what we were saying. But slowly, as the work progressed, he began to open more and more. He began to recognize how much his life-style and the way he was relating to women was a compensation for deep insecurities. While in the beginning, he was feeling superior to "all these people with so many problems," as he went deeper, he began to see that he was no different from everyone else. By the end, he felt like he was starting a new life. He was beginning to see how many of his old habits were destructive, how his relationships were superficial, and how little he really knew about himself. He left inspired and encouraged to start fresh.

But he was torn because he could not see how his old friends could accept his changing, or how his parents could love and accept him if he was no longer the person they wanted him to be and were accustomed to his being. They were so proud that he was successful and well respected and they were hoping that he would soon have a stable marriage and give them many grandchildren. He did not tell them that he was doing workshops, working with a therapist, and questioning many of the values that he had always accepted because he was sure that they would disapprove. For several years, he dropped out of therapy and stopping attending workshops. Then he contacted us again because he was experiencing panic attacks. He was having trouble focusing on his work and his boss became concerned with his performance. He began working with individual sessions again but once his panic symptoms diminished, he was sporadic in his commitment to continuing to do inner work.

Edward's situation is not uncommon with many people that we have known over the years. Often people are excited when they get a taste of inner work but when they become aware of the potential consequences of changing, they give up. Most of us are torn between growth and stability, between discovering our truth and maintaining the status quo. Furthermore, it takes tremendous courage to question the values we were raised with and to run the risk of facing disapproval and even rejection from our family. Separating is not easy.

We may become aware that our conditioning and our life are a prison, but to take the next step and separate from our past is quite another story. In the next portion of this book, we take up the process of separating and the fears and guilt involved in doing so.

The great German philosopher, Friedrich Nietzsche, described three different stages of evolving human consciousness. The first, he called the stage of the "camel." The "camel" is the stage of childhood conditioning where we assimilate the patterns, values, and behavior of our parents and our ancestors. As "camels," we are transmitted the wisdom of our past. But we also assimilate the unconsciousness, prejudices, and repression of those who raised us and those who came before us. As camels, we say "yes." We accept the teachings of the past without questioning them. But if we remain a camel forever, we remain stuck and there is no progression of consciousness.

Turkey is one of the countries where we present seminars and trainings. It is striking to us how much our participants there are still trapped in "the camel stage." Most of the men still traditionally treat women as emotional slaves and have conditioned expectations as to how they should be treated. Their behavior is often tyrannical and not infrequently violent, especially when their expectations are not met. The more progressive men are no longer aggressive but it is extremely difficult for them to understand, feel, and express any kind of vulnerability.

The women are equally as imbedded in their cultural upbringing. Their patterns of being compliant with men is quite automatic, even to the point where they don't question that women should expect or behave any differently. Many relate that they have been physically or emotionally abused by their fathers and witnessed fathers mistreating their mothers and their siblings. Those who have begun to do workshops and therapy are beginning to break out of these patterns of compliance and slavery but the trauma is profound. As one might expect, we have many more women participants than men in Turkey because it is still rare to find a man who is willing to open up and change. It is painful for us to observe and hear how much abuse women have experienced from men in their culture. We are slowly encouraging them to stand up for themselves and learn to feel and express their needs and to set limits.

Nietzsche calls the second stage of development the stage of the "lion." To make a leap forward, we have to move to the stage of the "lion," which rebels against the old. The lion says no! He or she questions the values and behavior of the past and what we have been taught. The lion roars against the repression, staleness, and security of the past, of the known and of the familiar. He breaks out of the bondage of tradition and courageously goes for the new.

Only by becoming a lion are we able to realize our true potential as a human being. It takes tremendous courage to move from the camel stage to the lion. The danger of the lion stage is that we can get stuck in that stage and get addicted to the energy of rage. If we remain as a lion, we can spend our lives roaring and even forming an identity as one who roars against authority or any kind of rules, blindly rebelling to everything.

Alex, a client of mine (Krish), exemplifies someone trapped in the lion stage. He has become a professional rebel. As a child, he experienced his father as distant, angry, and drunk much of the time. He ran away when he was thirteen and began living on the streets, eventually becoming involved in drugs and addicted to heroin. Fortunately, he recovered from his addiction but his life did not become any more stable. He had two children by two different women; left them both and lost contact with his ex-wives and his children. He went from one dysfunctional relationship to another, because he said that "settling down was just not in his blood."

It was a bit of miracle that he came to see me because he claimed that therapy and talking about himself and his childhood was "a waste of time." If I attempted to link his childhood experiences to his behavior in his life, he would simply laugh and say that I was "just trying to therapize him." Unfortunately, his rebellion toward any structure and all authority left him a desperately lonely man. But to take the risk, become vulnerable, and feel the pain he was holding inside did not seem a step that he either wanted or perhaps was capable of making. My impression was that he simply wanted someone to talk to but not to probe into his emotional pain. One day, he left a message on my machine canceling a session and I have not heard from him since.

According to Nietzsche, the stage of the "child" is the final stage of human consciousness. The child has transcended both "yes" and "no." There is neither the compliance of the camel nor the fight of the lion. The "child" is a deep opening to vulnerability.

In our experience, this process happens in two steps. The first is opening to the pain of our wounded vulnerability, of the loss of our innocence and trust. And in this process, we are willing to feel the grief of all that we have been through in our life. Once we are willing to go through this stage, the second happens on its own. It is a letting go of our fight with life and entering into a state of let go. We arrive at a state of acceptance of life and people as they are, but are still fully capable to use the strength of the lion whenever the situation calls for it. It is the return of innocence and trust, not the blind innocence and trust of the camel but the innocence of wisdom and maturity. This stage is what we call, "true forgiveness." It is not really "forgiveness" because we don't have to forgive anyone. We simply have arrived at a point where we see things as they are and accept them.

Nietzsche's Stages Describe the Process of Getting Out of Box

We begin to develop mature trust when we begin to trust and have confidence in ourselves again. In order to develop that self-trust, we need to discover who we are, and to do that, we have to step out of the box. The self-identity that we develop while growing up in the box is not in synchronicity with our being. To value ourselves, have an ability to make intelligent choices and find our unique expression as a person, it is important to move out of the influence and pressure of the old and expose ourselves to new ways of thinking and living.

As a "camel," we cannot trust ourselves. We compromise continuously in the name of harmony and therefore cannot develop mature trust. In the process of separating, we need to question everything that was taught us to discover for ourselves what is true and how to live authentically. In the box, we do not question. That is the life of the camel. The beauty of the camel is that we develop roots, a heritage and a sense of belonging. This will always be with us and in time, we can treasure these gifts. But until we have separated, they are a prison; our values are unquestioned. What we believe and how we behave is unconscious and we are unconscious.

In the initial stages of separating, it may feel as if we are going against the whole world and it can be helpful to get support from like-minded "lions." This phase of the lion can show itself in different ways. Some of us are more radical and dramatic and the movement of our "lion" energy is to overtly create a distance to physically separate from those who raised us. For others, the phase of the "lion" may be more subtle. It can be with surreptitious acts of defiance, sabotage, or resentment. We may not even realize that we are rebelling but our behavior is clearly a reaction to structure, convention, conformity, and authority.

Sometimes this period of rebellion may not begin until well into our adult life. But it is never too late. Instead of reacting to our primary caretakers, we may defy other authority figures or rebel against our cultural and religious repression. We have participants who become "lions" only after their children are grown and they have begun to break out of a marriage and an unquestioned lifestyle that was dead for a long time. The important thing in this phase is to recover our strength just as if we were to wake up a sleeping lion. The more conscious we are of this process, the healthier it is.

Alicia had an angry father and her husband behaved much the same way as her father did. We asked her if she ever felt angry when her husband yelled at her or stormed around the house in one of his tantrums.

"Oh, no." she responded. "I wouldn't want to be angry with anyone."

"If you could have," we asked, "what might you have said to him?"

"I would have asked him why he was so angry all the time."

"Would that have helped you feel stronger and not so victimized by his rage attacks?"

"No, probably not."

"OK," we said, "Tell us the most powerful person you can think of."

"Well, I guess that would be a girlfriend of mine who is never afraid to say how she feels."

"Ok," we suggested, "imagine that she is standing next to you, and your husband is in one of his rage attacks. What would she say or do?"

"She would tell him to shut up and take his anger somewhere else!"

"Good, how does it feel inside when you hear yourself saying that?"

"It feels strong and hot in my belly."

"Is it a good feeling?"

"Yes, it feels that if I could feel this I would feel better about myself."

"Do you think saying that to your husband when he is raging is bad or wrong?"

"No, not at all. He needs to hear that."

At this point, we are helping Alicia to discover her lion inside, a subject we will take up in the next chapter.

Naturally, there may be situations where it is not safe to assert the lion energy. For instance if someone is violent; then the lion energy is needed to take us away from that situation.

It is only once we develop some confidence in our lion and we can stand up for ourselves, that we are able to recover self-trust. The lion helps us to make life and daily decisions based not on what we were conditioned to believe and do, but on what feels true to our soul.

When this process of separating begins and we start to have a sense of ourselves again we naturally move into the final stage, that of the "child." We rediscover our innocence—an innocence that is tested and matured because we found the courage to be a "lion." But as a "child," we drop the anger and resentment of the "lion." It is no longer needed and it no longer feels right inside. Our heart and our nature do not like to hold on to anger and resentment. Furthermore, we are now free to rediscover our past in a new light. We can start to appreciate the beauty and richness of our heritage without the unconsciousness and repression that went with it. We can re-embrace the sense of belonging that it gives us and the wisdom that it holds. It no longer has the power to enslave us.

In our experience, the transition through these three stages is not linear. In some areas of our life and with some people, we may feel the innocence and maturity of the "child." But in other areas, we may still be deeply immersed in the unconsciousness of the "camel," or the defiance of the "lion." However, having the perspective of these stages makes it easier to watch the process with compassion and understanding. In the next chapter, we take up the process of separating in greater detail.

Exercise:

Ask yourself:

1. *How am I holding myself back because I am afraid of what others might think or say?*

2. *In what ways am I compromising in my life?*

3. *What was I taught about anger? Are there situations where anger is appropriate?*

4. *In what ways is my connection to my parents and family jeopardizing my growth as a person?*

* * *

CHAPTER 7:

THE POWER IN SEPARATING –

Breaking and Reconnecting with Our Roots

Your way begins on the other side.
Become the sky.
Take an axe to the prison wall,
Escape,
Walk out like someone born into color.
Do it now.
Rumi

Separating from our roots is possibly the most powerful and empowering growth step we will ever take and perhaps the most frightening and challenging one as well. It is frightening because the terrors of being punished, cast off from family and friends and finding no new identity to replace the one we are attempting to dissolve are very great. At the same time, we also know deep inside that going through this process of separating and finding ourselves (it is called separation and individuation) is vital.

It is as though there are two sides of us moving in opposite directions. One side is pushing us to break away and find ourselves, while another side is pushing us to preserve the comfort and security of the known and familiar. The interesting point is that when we have not consciously separated from our roots, we continue to play out this process of separation with the significant people in our lives today, and this can be extremely damaging to the relationships.

Re-examining Our Values

Not long before I (Krish) was about to graduate from college, I was visiting a friend who lived down the hall from me. It was just weeks before we all were leaving and after living together for so long, we were each going our own way. It seemed that most people I knew were planning to continue schooling in some form. But when I walked into this friend's room, I was surprised to notice that it didn't look at all as though he was getting ready to go to graduate school or any school for that matter. He had climbing gear spread all over the place. I asked him what his plans were and he told me that he didn't really know. He said he needed a break from this academic world and that he was considering going mountain climbing in Nepal and then just doing nothing on a beach in Thailand.

At first, that seemed really crazy to me. Good for him, maybe, but not for me. Or was it? What he said affected me and I kept thinking about it. Before then, I was sure that after graduation, I would go on to medical school. I had applied, been accepted, and that was the agenda that my family and conditioning dictated for me. It had never even occurred to me that I could or even wanted to "get off the train." But my friend had planted a seed. When I walked up to get my diploma, the dean asked me what my plans were. In spite of all the pomp and circumstance of a Harvard graduation ceremony, the words that came out were—"I don't really know." My family was shocked. My brother, who by then was a third year medical student, asked me why I didn't say that I was going to medical school. Feeling guilty and insecure, all I could say to him was that it just seemed like the honest thing to say at the time. Intuitively, I must have known that it was not right for me to go to medical school at this time in my life.

I was confused and disturbed. I started medical school because I still was not courageous enough to step off the train of my conditioning. After three weeks, I dropped out. It was one of the most difficult decisions of my life. I was going against all that I had been taught and trained for. My father, knowing how hard it was to get accepted to medical school, feared that I was ruining my chances. I suspected that he might be right but I had no choice. Terrified and confused, I got into my car and drove to the West Coast.

I began a time when I felt totally lost, depressed, and without direction. I joined the domestic Peace Corps, spent a couple of years working in black ghettos, and then went to California and became a hippie for three years. I lived in communes, experimented with psychedelic drugs, met and lived with people and in situations that caused me to question many of the beliefs I was raised with. I began practicing yoga and meditation and doing individual therapy and growth workshops, connecting with the shame and pain that I was carrying inside, which had roots in my childhood.

I lost the fantasy I was carrying of my "perfect upbringing" and began to see that what I had been taught was in fact driven, judgmental, and insanely slanted toward achievement and goal orientation. I recognized how much shaming and pain I had been through in trying to adjust to these values. Our conditioning is very deep and unconscious and in my inner search, I needed to confront deeper and deeper layers to investigate what was real for me and what was just habit. This process continues even today because there are deeper and more subtle layers to question.

The Right Climate for Change

Existence seems to throw us little opportunities to help us separate. It is not easy to say what makes us ready, but it seems to be some combination of inner and outer circumstances. Inside, we may reach a point, as I did, where we are fed up and search for something else. Then support may come in the form of a glimpse of something else, something new and different.

I (Amana) met a new friend when I was sixteen who became a catalyst in opening my eyes to a different world. The first time I visited her home, I was shocked at how opposite it was to my own. Her apartment was almost empty, except for some pictures of Buddhist monks and pictures of Tibet, just bare wooden floors and not very comfortable furniture. Her mother was a Buddhist nun who spent most of her time in retreats in India and France. By contrast, the home I grew up in was very comfortable and carpeted and didn't have the same spacious feeling. As our friendship developed, something deep inside me stirred; almost like recognizing something I had known earlier and had been missing I realized that I couldn't find what I was looking for if I stayed in Denmark with my family. I had to get away to experience life elsewhere to get some perspective. Furthermore, I didn't like the person I was becoming and it felt like if I stayed I would be following a script already written and living a life that would not be my own.

Up until that time, I had been spending most of my time reading, and I was at the top of my class throughout school. I could read fluently at the age of five and would always read instead of play. I spent most of my time at the local library and at around age twelve had started to question the way in which the grown-ups were living. I didn't like what I saw and could see no thrill in living life if this was all there was. My family had no connection to any kind of spirituality—no feeling or concept of anything higher than an ordinary, mundane existence, no soul searching or deeper inquiry into life and no idea of human development. They went to church only for baptisms, confirmations, weddings, and funerals and even then it was all about the parties, the food, and the gathering of the family. There was no sense of any connection to the church and nobody listened to the priest. I grew up with a deep sense that something was missing and I didn't know what.

One day, I came home from school and told my mother that I was quitting high school and going to Spain with my friend. Naturally, she freaked out and tried all kinds of ways to get me to change my mind but I was determined and a few weeks later, I left. Spain was the opposite of Denmark. Denmark was rational, controlled, reasonable, and even-tempered; Spain was passionate, hot, intense, and emotional. In Denmark, I had become very disconnected from my body and emotions and I knew that I needed to open up this part of me. We flew to Majorca and almost immediately moved into a totally new and exciting life-style. We easily found jobs and an apartment. Most nights, we would be out dancing till dawn at discos and we began meeting men.

I started to feel alive for the first time since I was a small child. During this time, the most amazing thing happened—my eyesight corrected. At the age of seven, at the time just before my parents separated, I had become very nearsighted and needed to wear thick glasses. Now, I suddenly noticed that I didn't need glasses or contact lenses any longer. What I really needed was to get away from the family, to get away from the role I was playing of being the responsible serious one. It was such a relief to be in a country where no one knew me and I could start all over. This new life opened my horizons to the point of not needing glasses anymore.

I later returned to Denmark to study but it was with a very different feeling inside.

The Significance of Breaking Contact

We may begin our separation by separating physically from our family of origin. We may even begin earlier than that by rebelling. Or it may happen by our sensing that there is something that calls us outside of the conventional world that we are familiar with. But these initial moves against or away from our roots only start the process of separation. One of the reasons that Nietzsche's stages are so brilliant is that it points out clearly that rebellion or physical separation is not really a separation but only an intermediate stage.

> *For the separation to become integrated and deep, we have to begin to find ourselves as unique individuals and then slowly make peace with all that came before. Until then, we either are in denial of or in reaction to our past.*

This does not happen simply by being physically separate (although that is often a good start) nor does it happen if we are in reaction to our past (although that too is necessary in the beginning of separating.)

Sometimes the first significant step we take away from our conditioning may be to physically separate from our parents and family and break contact for a time. This in itself is difficult and frightening. We discover in our work that it is very common for adults to be still living with or strongly connected emotionally to their parents; they don't the price they are paying.

In a workshop, a man in his early forties shared that he was having continual fights with his girlfriend because she complained that she felt the energy of his mother around him all the time. His mother bought his clothes, decorated his apartment, and they spoke on the phone nearly every day. Still, he could not see why this was a problem or why it was disturbing his girlfriend. When we first pointed out to him how deeply bonded he was to his mother and how it was affecting his relationship, he became defensive and angry. With time, he began to see how strongly his life was still being controlled by his mother's influence and intrusiveness. A few months later, he told his mother that she was not to come and visit him unless she was invited and he did not want her to make comments about his home or his life unless he asked. It took tremendous courage for him to take this step and through this decision he began to feel stronger and more confident, although at first extremely guilty and scared We have to face a lot of fear and guilt when we separate; as it feels like betraying our parents.

The Bonding to Our Family of Origin is Subtle and Powerful

The ties that bind us to family and parents are subtle and enormously powerful. Even when we are physically separated, the influence is still strong, particularly if we have not yet discovered our own values and do not yet trust our own intelligence. As long as we are still living the life that we were conditioned to live and believe the values, standards, and rules we were taught, we compromise and don't even realize the extent to which this compromise affects our lives.

A thirty-year-old man in a recent seminar was sharing with us that he is very close to his mother. His mother calls him nearly every day to see how he is doing but also to complain to him about her relationship with his father. He feels very guilty if he isn't able to give her the time and interest that he feels she deserves. At first, he thought that this was a normal situation but could not understand why he was having such trouble in his relationships with women. It became more evident as we went on that he felt he was betraying his mother if he opened deeply to another woman or even had sex with a woman. We encouraged him to begin to take steps to separate from his mother.

After the workshop was over, he spoke to her and explained that he needed to take distance from her for his own inner growth. She seemed to accept this well but two days later, called him to complain about how bad she felt about his decision. He felt horribly guilty and wavered in his decision. Several days after this phone call, his father called to ask him how much longer he was going to continue with "this nonsense" because he should realize how much he was hurting his mother.

There are deeper and deeper layers to explore in our process of separation. Even once we have begun to live our own lives, the hooks may still be extremely powerful. So much of our personality is affected that we often can't recognize the ways that we are behaving in habitual ways and holding on to beliefs about ourselves.

Many years ago, we were in Rome. All the shops were closed because it was a holiday but one was open by the Trevi fountain. Amana noticed a beautiful men's sweater in the window and suggested that I try it on. I told her that I didn't need any more sweaters. And anyway, it was too expensive. My conditioning says that any article of clothing over $100 is prohibitive and anyway, "one shouldn't buy anything which one doesn't need." But I am also a bit of a "clothes horse" so it didn't take Amana much to persuade me to buy that sweater. As soon as I left the shop, I got a massive attack from my inner judge. "You didn't need that! You already have too much weight in your suitcase! That was a terrible waste of money! You are distracting yourself from your spiritual search with so many material things!" and so on. All the way back to where we were staying I went on and on but fortunately by then, I had enough space from this powerful judge not to take it too seriously. I could recognize that it was my family's values that were being threatened by this "extravagance."

And to illustrate how conditioning runs in the family, I (Krish) notice that even today my older brother, in spite of his position as a leading authority in his field of neuro-ophthalmology, is very reluctant to spend money on anything that he considers frivolous. His pants are chronically too short and most of his clothes have been around since we were in high school together. Forget eating out at expensive restaurants.

Separating Requires Risk

The most powerful step we can take in separating from the limitations of our conditioning is to take risks. More precisely, it means risking to do something our heart would love to do but our conditioning has told us is wrong. Or risking doing something we were told we couldn't do or were not good at. This kind of risking brings tremendous empowerment. It releases massive amounts of energy trapped in our system and expands our vision and sense of ourselves. Through the journey of risking, our identity begins to shift away from a shamed unworthy person to a capable unique person.

When we speak about risk, we do not mean foolhardy acts of daring. On the contrary, we mean very precise risks that directly challenge our conditioning such as:

1. *Risk expressing our creativity and allowing ourselves to be seen in spite of the fear of humiliation, disapproval, or rejection.*

2. *Risk feeling and expressing our feelings, sexuality, and life energy rather than staying hidden.*

3. *Risk being angry and confronting someone whom we feel has been disrespectful to us.*

4. *Risk being vulnerable rather than having to be right.*

5. *Risk feeling afraid, helpless, and insecure and sharing these feelings.*

6. *Risk learning to feel what we want and need and learning to give that to ourselves.*

7. *Risk opening up and feeling the pain and disappointment when others or life are not how we want them to be.*

8. *Risk discovering our own way of parenting instead of following blindly how we were raised.*

9. *Risk being honest.*

10. *Risk living our life the way we want to live it.*

11. *Risk saying no to something we before automatically said yes to.*

12. *Risk putting yourself first even if it means disappointing someone.*

13. *Risk listening and sincerely taking the other person into your heart.*

When We Stop Seeking Approval, the Circle is Completed

It is a significant milestone in our life when our self-esteem no longer depends on the love and approval of those who raised us. The wounded part in us may never let go of wanting the love and respect we didn't get. But at a certain point, we may discover that those we have turned to for this kind of nourishment cannot give it to us in the way we needed it. This is a valuable, deeply spiritual rite of passage. As long as we still *expect* something from those who raised us, we continue to come to them as a child and we are trapped in the same net. We will come away feeling shamed, tired, depressed, not loving ourselves, and once again having reinforced our shamed self-image.

The process of weaning ourselves of our addiction for approval comes from listening to our intuitive wisdom. It is giving us signals all the time and when we listen, something begins to feel right inside when we live according to our truth.

Learning to listen and feel the inner voice that guides us on our authentic path is a bit like making deposits in a bank. At first, it is small account and doesn't have much clout. With time, as the account grows, the voice gets louder, and it is easier to feel what it is like inside when we follow this intuition, this inner feeling of "rightness." As this process deepens, we are able to stop turning to others and particularly to those who raised us for advice about how to live our life. Our hearts can open to them because we no longer allow others to distract us. When we don't come as a beggar but as a giver, we may even have tremendous gratitude for what we did receive. And we may be able to see our parents for the people they are, with all their limitations and defects; as human beings doing the best they can.

A close friend of ours who also, like Krish, came from an enmeshed Jewish family upbringing, suffered for years because he felt that his father never approved of him. In his early twenties, he went to England to study acupuncture but sensed that his father would have been more proud of him had he taken up Western medicine. After his studies, he left for India and became a disciple of an enlightened spiritual master, living for years in his commune there, another move that his father was not too crazy about. His desperate need for the approval of his father manifested itself in seeking approval from other authority figures and he continually felt that he was being slighted, unrecognized, and unsupported.

He kept battling with this conflict for many years but finally, something dramatic shifted inside him. He found the courage to truly live according to his own inner direction. His acupuncture practice is now booming and he is beginning to feel proud of himself as a person. On the two most recent visits with his father, he noticed that he was no longer seeking his approval as strongly as in the past and, paradoxically, his father told him several times how proud of him he was.

The Last Phase of Separation – Honoring Our Past

The roar of the lion is not what brings back our self-respect and our trust. Rebellion is like a booster rocket that gives us the strength to break away. But the real empowerment comes when we find ourselves separate from our roots and start to live according to our inner voice rather than to the countless outer voices we may have listened to in the past. Only then can we truly honor what we have learned and received from our roots. Our heart does not want to stay with rancor and enmity. These emotions hurt and it create separation. But we have to allow this period of separation and pain however long it takes.

I (Amana) had to have a long period where I was not having any contact with my mother in order to separate. It was painful and difficult but necessary for me to begin to feel myself again separate from her. I had lost touch with the inner sense of myself and had adapted to playing a role of the responsible adult-child in the family. It was painful to separate because my mother is such a truly loving person and she could not understand what I was going through. I was angry at her for not giving me what I needed, I was even angry at her for not wanting more from life than the life she was living. I could not understand how she could be happy with that. She kept saying: "You are just like your father. Never satisfied with what you have." It hurt me to hear that and at the same time, I could understand her fear that I would become like my father and give up on life.

I wasn't able to understand that she couldn't give to me what I needed and she didn't have the same spiritual longing as I did. It has taken me many years to accept and see her for who she is, and today I really appreciate her and honor her for everything she is and for what she has given me. She has a very loving heart and has given me a basic trust in life that I know I wouldn't have had had it not been for her.

As we grow out of the rebellion, we begin to feel gratitude for those who came before us and see them for who they are. We can even accept what we went through as a gift in spite of the difficulty and the pain we experienced. We can reconnect with our roots and with the people who raised us and receive them in a different way. In many conscious and unconscious ways, our lives, our destiny, and our personalities are deeply patterned around our parents and the culture we were raised in. Once we have separated, we can appreciate that the apple has fallen both very far from and very close to the tree.

Whether or not we like it or are aware of it, we are carrying on the torch in many ways. We may notice more and more how much we are like one or both of our parents. We find ourselves thinking, acting, and talking like them in ways that we never realized before. In the past, I was totally uninterested in politics and never bothered to vote. But when my father died, I (Krish) suddenly discovered that I was as deeply concerned about social injustice as he was. I also inherited some of negative traits as well such as his fierce independence and his ability to shut out the outside world and everyone around him. We may like some of the ways we resemble our parents and we may not like others; in either case, it is part of who we are. This is true not only about our parents but also about the cultural heritage we come from. The completion involves becoming aware of our heritage, accepting it and even finding strength from it.

With separation and reconnection, we complete the circle of our healing process. We have gone through the dark tunnel, allowing ourselves to feel, from the perspective of the wounded inner child, the wounds we sustained while we were small. And we have found the courage to separate from our roots in order to find out who we are. Having taken that part of the journey, we can also discover the ways we are deeply connected to our past and embrace with gratitude what we have inherited. In this way, we neither reject the pain of the past nor cling to it. Then we are able to appreciate that what we have been through has only deepened and enriched us.

Exercise:

Ask yourself:

1. *In what ways do I think and behave like my father and my mother?*

2. *In what ways am I different?*

3. *In what ways do my interests, hobbies, and habits resemble theirs?*

4. *In what ways am I still carrying the beliefs of my cultural and religious upbringing?*

5. *In what ways have I changed my ideas from this conditioning?*

* * *

PART 3:

LIFE LESSONS
FOR LEARNING TRUST

CHAPTER 8:

EMPOWERMENT –

The Life Lesson of Retrieving Our Integrity

The way of the heart is the way of courage.
It is to live in insecurity;
Courage is to move on dangerous paths.
A person who is alive, vitally alive, will always move into the
unknown.
There is danger there, but he will take the risk.
The head always calculates – the heart is non-calculating.
Osho

There are some specific and practical steps we can take for learning real trust. One, as we have mentioned, is the process of separating from our roots and finding our individuality. Another is learning to stand up for ourselves, for our dignity and for our truth.

A forty-two-year-old woman in a recent seminar was sharing with us that her sexual relationship with her husband was not going smoothly. She felt that he approached her to make love in a way that made her feel rushed and overrun. When she said that she didn't want to make love, he became hurt and pulled away and when she said that she needed more time and caring in their lovemaking, he told her that he wanted her sexual energy not her emotional problems.

"How do you feel when he says this to you?" we asked.

"I think he is probably right. I also think that sometimes I am too sensitive and emotional."

She judges herself, trying as best she can to comply with his sexual needs but then feels depressed and resentful afterward.

"What would it be like if you made love the way you would like?" we asked.

"I can't even imagine what that would be like."

Perhaps many of us can relate to similar situations in our own lives in which we are not able to connect with or to affirm our own needs and wishes. We may not even know what we need, we are so used to adapting to people around us, and we say and do things that we don't mean. One of the fundamental reasons that we have so little trust in others is that many of us feel disempowered in our dealings with life and with people. We easily give in to others and feel intimidated, particularly if there is a threat of confrontation or abandonment. This makes us lose dignity and self-respect, but we feel helpless and we blame ourselves harshly for not being stronger or we blame others for not respecting us or being more sensitive to us.

The issue of empowerment is perhaps one of the most vital we face in life. Without a sense of mastery—an ability to navigate in life with some degree of confidence, dignity, and self-respect, we can easily feel victimized and collapsed. When we feel powerless and victimized, it wears away at our self-esteem and we don't see the options we have to change the situation. In the example above, the husband is not the reason for her difficulties. If she were with another man, most likely she would encounter the same situation.

For the sake of harmony and getting love from another, we go along with what others want. It is hard to assert our needs when we don't even know what they are or even if we do, we are too terrified to assert them. Sometimes, we discover in retrospect that we did not stand up for ourselves or allowed another to overstep our boundaries but it seems too late. It is pointless to tell ourselves that next time, we are going to assert ourselves because often, when it happens, we are not aware that we have overstepped ourselves or were overstepped by someone until later—sometimes much later.

We are torn inside between the longing to open and trust and the passion to feel strong and become a master of ourselves; between the longing to be loved and the desire to be true to ourselves.

Often, the closer we come to someone, the more extreme this conflict becomes. We attempt to cope with a chronic feeling of disempowerment in one of two ways. Either we isolate ourselves, feel continually suspicious and on guard, hold everyone at a distance and do not allow ourselves to be vulnerable. Or, as in the example of the woman above, we comply, lose ourselves, and give up our own needs.

In isolation, we numb ourselves to the pain of being disempowered. In the second case, our hunger for love and attention invites someone to come in without regard to our own needs or feelings. Neither of these two coping mechanisms brings us any closer to feeling a sense of mastery.

We sometimes ask people we work with to take some moments and reflect on what helps them to feel more empowered in their lives. Most commonly, they say such things as:

"I feel empowered when I feel centered."
"I feel empowered when I can set limits."
"I feel empowered when I take responsibility for myself."
"I feel empowered when I am not such a coward."
"I feel empowered when I know what I need to say or do."

"I feel empowered when I realize how committed I am to my growth and how far I have come."

"I feel empowered when I succeed."

"I feel empowered when I am connected to my body and feel grounded with the earth."

Based on these statements, it is clear that we feel empowered when we are able to "be in our energy" but we feel disempowered when we feel helpless, confused, and overpowered by life or someone else. Yet we are being unkind to ourselves when we base our empowerment simply on the times when we feel centered, strong, and assertive. When we have been wounded in our self-esteem, as many of us have, much of the time we are too shocked to be able to feel ourselves and to respond appropriately. And often, we are so out of touch with what we want, need, feel, and think, that we discover only later that we have betrayed ourselves.

From our experience, we learn empowerment by saying yes to ourselves on a deep level. That means feeling ourselves with a quality of compassion and accepting whatever we find inside each moment. From that space, our truth and our strength bubble up spontaneously.

The Two Poles of Empowerment

We find that there are two aspects to empowerment—one is what we refer to as the female pole and the second is the male pole:

1. The Female Aspect of Empowerment

This involves **observing and feeling** ourselves closely in those moments when we feel threatened, helpless, intimidated, powerless, confused, paralyzed, frightened, insecure, and/or collapsed. We observe and feel without the expectation or pressure that we will be able to respond powerfully or even be able to respond at all. The shock may be so profound that all we can do in the moment is simply observe the whole situation.

This means becoming aware of and feeling the *fears* that are provoked, particularly when another person wants something from us or when we feel overwhelmed by life's challenges. Normally, in these situations, we are not present; we space out in one way or another by complying, withdrawing, or dissociating. It takes a great deal of courage to be present and to feel what is happening inside. It is hard to imagine how deep the fears are.

The empowerment comes from finding the courage and commitment to stay present and feel the fear and the subtle body sensations associated with the fear. In the example we gave in the beginning of the chapter, if this woman allowed herself to feel the fear in the moment when she is making love and feel how her husband provokes that fear, she would begin to develop respect for herself. In the beginning, she may not recognize it as fear. It may show itself as a feeling of sadness, pain, and disconnection from her husband, no desire for lovemaking, anxiety, or depression.

Slowly, with time and patience, we learn to notice in these frightening situations not only that we are a panicked child but also that we have the strength and commitment to feel ourselves rather than space out. Through trial and error, and without pressure to "do it right," when we commit to staying present and feeling, we begin to discover **what feels right to us and what does not.**

The Male Pole of Empowerment

This involves **taking small risks** to say what we need and want even if we run the risk of anger, disapproval, or judgment from another. It also involves committing to taking small steps in not allowing our fears to cause us to sink into procrastinating and withdrawal. This is what a psychologist friend of ours calls, "spiritual stretching." Again, it is not a question of doing or saying the right thing but of simply taking a risk to behave in a way that is new and different and closer to our heart—to do something that we were too afraid of doing.

Taking small risks is immensely transformative—they produce a deep inner change. That change is empowerment. Gradually our fears diminish and our inner sense of self returns.

Another important aspect of the male pole is to do something that brings more life energy and awareness into the body. We call it "the move your ass factor." This can include sports, martial arts, dance, body awareness exercises, lifting weights, spending time in nature, playing a musical instrument, painting—whatever inspires us and brings us joy. Anything that helps us become more grounded and connected to our body will allow us to stay more present in the moments when we feel threatened by someone or by some situation.

Sometimes in life, we are in a situation in which we can use only the female pole. Other times, we can do both. A client of ours recently had two interesting situations in her life that challenged her to work with empowerment. In the first situation, she went home to visit her family for a month. After a few days in her parents' house, she felt herself becoming extremely disturbed. She was irritated at everything her parents said and did and she felt herself becoming more and more insecure. Furthermore, she felt powerless to say or do anything to make herself feel stronger and better inside. Her father had always been verbally and emotionally abusive with her as a child and her mother was unsupportive. Our client noticed that after a few days, she had regressed deeply into her childhood state. Yet she was able to stay present with the feelings of fear and shame and she knew that soon she would be leaving and returning to her regular life far from her parents.

When she returned home, she encountered a situation that presented her with another challenge. She works in a spa as a reflexologist. Before she left, she trained another of the massage therapists to do reflexology to fill the time that she was away with the understanding that when she returned, she would continue to be the sole reflexologist. But when she returned, she discovered that the owners of the spa were referring clients to him instead of calling her because he spent more hours there and was more quickly available. She felt betrayed and felt that his short two-week training did not compare to her years of studying for this work. She confronted the owners of the spa who supported her and reinstated her as the sole reflexologist. In the first case with her parents, she could work only with the female pole of empowerment because she was too regressed and shocked to do anything else. In the second, she could move to the male pole and actually confront the situation by putting out her needs and wants. In both cases, she empowered herself.

> *The most important thing to understand about empowerment is that if we do not accept our fears (the female pole) then we cannot move toward the male pole of taking risks.*

The risk-taking has to come out of a deep acceptance of our fears and insecurities. The foundation of empowerment is the deep inner feeling that nothing is wrong even though there is so much fear.

The Three Stages of Empowerment

It is natural and instinctual that when we feel unjustly treated or if one of our basic needs in life is threatened, we get angry. But many of us have lost this essential skill. The anger that we would feel in these moments is a natural reaction to defend our integrity. For instance, if we feel disrespected, and are able to feel and express our displeasure forcibly, it would restore our dignity. But if we are unable to respond in this way, we are left feeling helpless, powerless, deeply humiliated, and shamed. This ability to defend ourselves is a natural healthy energy that many us have lost because we were not supported to stand up for ourselves in this way, and it might have been much too dangerous to do so. We might even have seen one of our parents take constant abuse and never respond with dignity.

Stage 1: Validating and Feeling Our Shock and Our Fears – Our Protector Has Not Yet Woken up

At first, most of us are disconnected from our ability to stand up for ourselves, to set limits; sometimes to even realize that we have lost our power. We may experience intrusion, invasion, disrespect, and even abuse without realizing that we are being mistreated. Some of us, because of our past, have become accustomed to being humiliated and abused one way or another.

For instance, I (Krish) was frequently teased and put down by my older brother when I was younger and got used to feeling small and humiliated. It felt almost like a second skin. Only later, when I began to learn about shame, did I realize that I had developed a shame identity and expected to be treated in this way. This identity went so deep that even today, I still can hardly believe when I am successful in my life. To develop the ability to recognize when I am being mistreated is still not easy. Through therapy and workshops, over time, I was able to find the place inside that would no longer tolerate and no longer felt I deserved disrespect of any kind. Yet, it is still not easy to recognize in the moment when it is appropriate to set a limit.

> *The first step, therefore, in learning the life lesson of empowerment is to honor and respect our shock, shame, and fears.*

In a workshop we do on healing from shock and trauma, we do an exercise to help participants discover more about their wounded ability to set limits. They take a piece of string and make a circle around themselves wherever they feel their limits. Then they ask the person with whom he or she is doing the exercise to represent someone important in that person's life either in the present or in the past. The person approaches, and at some point, when it feels right, he or she says, "Stop!" The person feels the energy of the "Stop!" and the other person explains how he or she experienced the "No!" Sometimes people discover that there is no energy in their expression of "No!" as if they do not have the right to say it. Or they may not even be able to say no. Other times, they discover that their placement of the string does not correspond to their actual sense of their boundary. It may be where they would like it to be but not where it actually is.

Some people discover that their boundary is inside their body and the other person is free to invade them. They have allowed themselves to be invaded so much that they are unable to protect their own body from invasion. Others set their limits far outside and are terrified to let anyone near them. Most often it becomes clear with this exercise that we have either adapted to invasion by either always saying yes or always saying no. When we are wounded, we have not learned what it means to be present and to feel whether our truth is to say yes or no in the moment. We have never learned to respond according to our own feelings and according to the present moment.

The exercise also helps people to recognize the pure terror that they feel when the person who is approaching represents someone who has invaded them in the past. The process of learning to respect our needs and our limits again is slow and sometimes discouraging because we are so deeply frightened. We learn by taking the smallest risks to begin to feel that we have the right to stand up for ourselves and that we won't die of loneliness or aggression when we do. Each little step in this direction builds strength and an inner sense of self.

Our healing at this stage is to learn **to honor** and **to feel** the shock. The shock is very deep. In the moment when we are taken over by shock and terror, it is extremely difficult to stand up for ourselves in the way that we would like. To berate ourselves for not being able to do this is not much help. Depending on our past, certain people may terrify us. And when we are around people today who remind us of those people, we may simply feel small, powerless, unsafe, insecure, worthless, and useless. This situation rekindles an early wound and in their presence, we regress.

Becoming Aware of What We Feel and Think

When we have been traumatized and conditioned how to think and what to feel, many of us have abandoned our integrity long ago. Most of us could write five books on all the things that we "should have said." We can be totally brilliant, articulate, and empowered in retrospect but at the moment when an invasion or disrespect occurs, we can be numb and compliant. Furthermore, because we lost our integrity and feel so bad inside, many of us invite disrespect. We may have cultivated a pleasing personality just to smooth things over and try to make the world a little safer. And now we may even judge ourselves for being so pleasing and compliant. To abandon that role and become honest, direct, and confrontational is extremely challenging.

Recently, we rented a little beach cabin in Byron Bay, Australia, and because it was the high season, the cost of the rental was very high. When we arrived, I (Amana) noticed immediately that the place was dirty but neither of us said anything. We didn't want to offend the managers who had just finished "cleaning" as we arrived. The next day, we discovered that the DVD player was not working and we love to watch movies, particularly when we are not working and have extra time. We called the managers and asked if they could get it fixed.

Days went by before it was taken care of and we began to feel more and more resentful that we were paying such a high rent for a place that was dirty and uncared for. We could both see how our "nice person" personalities, which were saying, "Oh, why make such a fuss!" and "It's only for a short time!" and so on were making it difficult for us to stand up and confront the situation. We finally managed to make it absolutely clear that we wanted that DVD player fixed NOW. The owners actually came through, apologizing and offering to let us to stay an extra day free. We learned some valuable things from the whole experience. For one, we both have "good person" personalities that are afraid of making anyone upset or troubled. But we also have high standards and it is no longer OK for us to stay in places that don't live up to those standards. Finally, we learned that it is not only fine but also really important to express our discontent.

Much of our rage when we feel disrespected is actually anger toward ourselves for not taking the time to feel and honor what we want and need. Many of us are so traumatized that we have to learn to listen to ourselves again. To do that, it is important to slow things down enough so that we can feel again. Trauma and invasion cause our nervous system to speed up—we can become hypervigilant and hyperactive. This becomes even worse in situations when we are afraid of someone. In such moments, it is hard to feel ourselves. We have learned to say yes, to accept what others, especially authority figures, say as the truth.

We learn to go along with things because it is unimaginable not to. Therefore, before we can even imagine setting appropriate limits and standing up for what we feel, think, need, and perceive, we have to slowly and patiently begin to feel invasions when they occur.

Stage 2: Owning Our Rage – Waking Up Our Protector

At a certain point, with guidance and support, we start to realize what we have put up with. We start to tap into the well of resentment, hurt, and rage that we have stored inside for feeling too helpless to stand up for ourselves. These feelings may show themselves in countless ways – constant irritability, bouts of rage in inappropriate situations (like road rage), violence toward a child, a spouse, or an animal, or acts of revenge and spite. These are indirect and unconscious ways that our repressed anger shows itself.

A couple we have worked with have been in a relationship for five years. The woman's father was violent and physically abusive and she is still terrified and deeply mistrustful of men. Her boyfriend has rage attacks and has been physically abusive with girlfriends in the past. Until recently, she has been unable to express her hurt or anger with her boyfriend because she was too terrified of his reaction. Instead, she expressed her pent-up rage indirectly by withholding her love, criticizing him, and continually opposing him on details of living and working together.

She is gradually beginning to get in touch with the anger she has toward him for being abusive with her but even more importantly, she is beginning to feel her rage toward her father and all men for bullying women. Before she could connect with her rage, she needed to feel safe. She was able to express that she needed to have a commitment from him that no matter how much anger he feels, he would not be physically abusive toward her. When he told her sincerely that he would stand by that promise, it allowed her to fully express her rage. It was a huge step for her and a great relief.

In our experience, there is no alternative and no shortcut to feeling and expressing rage but we can learn to discharge the rage in ways in which we are not habitually throwing it on the other person. In our experience, getting into a habit of throwing rage at another person is destructive both to ourselves and to the relationship. It is much healthier to learn to discharge the anger through cathartic exercises in workshops, martial arts, kick boxing in a gym, or any work that encourages the expression of energy through sound and movement. I (Krish) benefited immensely from participating in workshops that supported my making friends with my rage. Now that I am more familiar with this energy, it is no longer necessary for me to do catharsis. Still, it is fantastic for me to express the energy on a regular basis by smacking a tennis ball. And now, when I am feeling anger about something or someone in my life, I can take walks and take time to feel it.

For some of us, the anger is repressed and for others of us, it is out of control, showing itself with chronic irritability and outbursts of anger with small provocations. We all have different childhood experiences and different ways that we adjusted to receiving or witnessing violence in our past. One person may become compliant and collapsed while another becomes more habitually tyrannical and rageful.

We had an incident in a recent workshop that was both shocking and touching. There were a large number of people in the room so we were not able to get to know each person's story. However, on the third (out of five) day, one of our assistants came to us and told us that a woman who were there with her husband had told her that on several occasions he had beaten her, once to the point of breaking her nose. We spoke to them privately to get the full story from both of them. He admitted that he had beaten her but he felt justified because she provoked him frequently by raging and screaming at him.

We decided at that point, that we needed to work with them first individually and then later to bring this up in the group at large. Amana spent an hour with her and Krish an hour with him. I (Krish) started by asking him to tell me in detail one exact incident when he had hit her.

"I came home and she was yelling at me for coming late."

"Where were you standing and where was she standing when this happened?" I asked.

"We were both in the kitchen and I was taking a beer out of the fridge."

"Then what happened?"

"I got angry and told her that I come home when I have to."

"How were you feelings at that moment?"

I felt pissed off. She doesn't consider me, she never considers me and I hate being yelled at!"

"Go on," I said, "tell me what happened next."

"She kept yelling and I got more and more angry and then I hit her in the face."

"What were you feeling at the moment you hit her?"

"Really pissed off."

"What else were you feeling?"

"Just angry, really angry."

"What else? Go deeper if you can."

"I was feeling helpless and cornered. I felt like I had nowhere to go."

"How does that feeling feel right now when you imagine that the whole thing is happening in this moment?"

"I feel very hot. I feel really tight in my chest."

"Are you aware of any fear?"

"Yes, I hate feeling helpless and I hate someone yelling at me!"

"Do you remember other times feelings like this from the past?"

"Yes, I felt like this when my father yelled at me."

We went on to explore this and he was able to feel deep pain of his father's abuse. I also worked with enabling him to see and feel the rage and shame for feeling so helpless and humiliated by his father.

Later, I asked him if he felt remorse about brutalizing his wife. (He was a very large man and even I could feel some fear for a potential outburst of his violence.)

"Yes, I do. But I have to tell you honestly, when I get angry, I can't control myself. I don't trust that anyone will respect me or my needs, ever."

"I understand that but I also have to tell you, that this kind of behavior is absolutely unacceptable. Are you willing to do whatever it takes to stop this behavior?"

"Yes. I love her and I know that this is going to destroy our relationship."

I (Amana) also worked with the woman to help her understand why she was provoking him and inviting his anger (her underlying rage with men) and to feel what was underneath (a story of sexual abuse as a child). She was feeling scared and lonely but unwilling to feel these feelings; she attacked him instead for coming home late.

I also helped her to learn to contain her feelings when he wasn't as available as she would like (the topic of the next chapter.) and to be gentler with her own needs and her abandonment.

The next day, we brought them together in front of the group. Many of the women had heard about what he had done and they were understandably disturbed. When he admitted to the whole group what he had done, it was very powerful for the women in the room who had also experienced and still experience violence from a man. But he was also able to feel the pain of what he had done, cried profusely, and made a solid commitment to her that he would never ever be violent with her. He also told everyone that he would seek whatever ongoing help he needed to learn to contain his anger. At this writing, it is two years since this incident. They have told us that he has not been violent again.

For some of us, we have to learn to embrace our anger again because we have repressed it. For others of us, it is more a question of learning to contain it. In both cases, we all have to learn to feel the fear, helplessness, and mistrust underneath. When we are disturbed, some of us move toward anger and attack, others toward collapse and compliance. Fear, helplessness, and mistrust are the root and need to be explored.

Stage 3 – Using Our Protector to Set Limits with Clarity and Centeredness

Once we develop some confidence in our ability to feel our needs and being able to express them clearly, we are entering into the third stage of the empowerment process. In this stage, we learn to use our protector to set limits when needed. In our work, we use an exercise to teach people this skill. We call it "cleaning house." After spending some time generating life energy and aliveness, we invite people to pick a partner and sit opposite each other. One person thinks of someone in his or her life with whom the person has felt mistreated, disrespected or abused.

We invite the person to say:

1. "I need to clear something up with you. Do you have the space to listen?" Having agreed, we suggest they go on say:

2. "It was/is really not OK for me when you did/do this…" and then the person can elaborate how he or she feels and what happens inside that is provoked by the other person's behavior. The first part of saying that "it is not OK" is very important because it communicates the limit energetically. We allow ourselves to feel the energy of anger but rather than throwing the anger at the other, we consciously channel it into a clear expression of a limit.

Owning our anger is the doorway to passion, power, and strength. This doesn't mean that we have to hold on to the anger forever. Once felt and owned, it paves the way for genuine forgiveness and protection of our vulnerability when needed.

> *We cannot authentically forgive until we have felt, from the perspective of our helpless child, the full extent of our betrayal. And when we connect with the rage, it is not to punish those responsible for violating our boundaries or to make them wrong. It is simply a process of waking up our sleeping inner strength and wisdom—a strength that knows what is right for us and knows how to protect ourselves when something threatens us.*

A man who came to a recent seminar was in the process of separating from his wife of twenty years. For most of their marriage, he played the role of the rescuer and she played the role of the helpless child. Slowly, he came to realize that this role was a restriction for him and he began to take steps to get out of being the rescuer. His wife objected vehemently, feeling betrayed and abandoned. Shortly prior to starting our workshop, he told her that he was going to attend our workshop and she said nothing. When he arrived to register, he was shocked to find that she had booked it as well without telling him.

We spoke to both of them before starting and he was willing to agree to allow her to participate as well but only on the condition that she did not interfere or relate to him in any way during the process. This was a huge step for him to make. As it turned out, they both grew immensely from the experience. She learned to give herself the space to be with her pain and loneliness and discovered a strength inside that she had not known before. He was able to expand with his newly found freedom and feel that he would not get punished for it. He learned that saying no was his right and it gave him much more inner strength.

The process of empowerment is not linear. We may take a step and respond in a new and stronger way, and then get an attack of primal panic and guilt, especially when our new behavior meets a negative reaction. Then we doubt ourselves and may feel that we did something horribly wrong. Saying yes to ourselves when it means saying no to another person brings up fears of rejection, punishment, and guilt of being selfish. We take a step forward and then perhaps we retreat in fear and guilt. Progress is gradual.

Baby Steps

The process of empowerment involves the risk of facing our fears, whatever they are. But in making a commitment to confront our fears, we also need to be deeply compassionate with ourselves. When we confront a fear such as being vulnerable, or allowing ourselves to be angry, or expressing what we want even when it goes directly against what someone close to us wants, we will be opening a primal terror.

There is no way to describe how terrifying this can be. If it does not bring up terror, chances are, it is not a real risk. There is good reason that we have spent a lifetime betraying ourselves, giving away our power, being nice when we didn't want to be nice, making compromises for crumbs of attention. That reason is pure terror to do anything else. When we begin to change this old ingrained pattern, we may be feeling fears that we never even knew we had. For that reason, we talk about "baby steps." Take risks, but make them small and give a lot of room for failure.

Life will provide us with ongoing opportunities to retrieve the integrity that we have lost. The most important step we can make in this process is simply being willing to continually observe and feel when we do not respect ourselves. Everything follows naturally from there. Once we make that commitment, it sets a process in motion that seems to gather momentum on its own. We become more aware of the ways we have compromised and continue to compromise our integrity. We develop understanding and compassion for the times we had no choice but to lose ourselves. We begin to forgive ourselves for the times when we are still too afraid and shocked to set boundaries. We become more sensitive to how our body feels when we have been invaded or when we have given ourselves away. And the more we feel how painful it is to compromise and abandon ourselves the more we find the strength inside to take steps to standing up for ourselves.

This process takes time and there is no way to do it "right." The idea that there is a "right" way to go about recovering our integrity only provides pressure and reinforces our shame of failure. Our body is a wonderful barometer for what is happening inside as we interact with people and the world outside. Fear and trauma have caused us to stop listening to our body signals and it takes some learning to discover this obvious treasure. When we take the time and the caring to listen, we discover that our body gives us signals when we feel safe, when there is a threat and if a certain situation or person is right for us or not. When our priority and focus are simply on listening to the body and not being so concerned if we say or do the "right" thing, set our boundaries, assert ourselves properly etc., then there is much less pressure. Each experience is a chance to learn to listen to ourselves.

When we begin to tune into these subtle signals inside, we also learn to trust our thoughts and our perceptions of the outside world, and we stop turning to others quite to compulsively to tell us what we feel, think, and should do. We become less mystified, less gullible, and less impressionable. It is important to understand that our ability to set a limit really has nothing to do with the other person. The other person does not have to change in any way. We reach a point when no matter what they say or do, we can no longer keep betraying ourselves and we are strong and mature enough to face the consequences.

Exercise:

Pick a situation in which you feel that someone has invaded you with aggression, disrespect for your space, blame, judgment, criticism, advice, or analysis.

Ask yourself:

1. *How do I feel inside in this moment?*

2. *How do I normally respond in the moment? Later?*

3. *Is it difficult for me to set boundaries with this person? What am I afraid of?*

4. *What could I imagine saying to this person or these people that would make me feel more empowered?*

5. *When I explode in anger, what are the deep fears inside?*

* * *

CHAPTER 9:

CONTAINMENT –

The Life Lesson of Letting Go

The agony of lovers
Burns with the fire of passion…
The wailing of broken hearts
Is the doorway to God.
Rumi

You have to encounter your emptiness
You have to live it, you have to accept it.
And in your acceptance is hidden a great revelation.
The moment you accept your aloneness,
It's very quality changes.
It becomes just its opposite –
It becomes an abundance, a fulfillment, an overflowing of energy
and joy.
Out of this overflowing,
if your trust arises, if your love arises,
it is not just a word, it is your very heart.
Osho

In a recent workshop, a woman shared that she was having difficulty in her relationship because she found that her man was not as present for her as she wanted. She loved him very much but she was frustrated because much of his behavior took him away from deep connection with her. She felt that he smoked too much, drank too much beer, watched too much TV, and ate too much. We helped her get in touch with the rage that she felt for him not being available for her and at a deeper level, also the rage that she had with her parents for not being present for her both in the past and now. But in terms of how to relate to her boyfriend, it was a delicate situation. Expressing her frustration toward him only made him more distant and it did not feel very creative for her to be angry and bitchy. There was something much deeper for her to learn than simply to get out her anger.

"What would it be like to accept him just the way he is?" we asked.

"If I do that, I will never get the love I need. He will just disappear into all his activities."

"What does it feel like if you accept that there is nothing you can do to change him and that your efforts to change him only make things worse?" we asked.

"It feels terrible. I can't accept that. I don't want to be with a man who is never there."

"Have you succeeded at changing him so far?"

"No."

"Do you love him enough to want to be with him even if he never changes?"

She thought about this question for a while. Finally, she said, "Yes, I think I do."

This situation is probably familiar. We find that there is something about the person we are close to, whether it is a lover or friend, that makes us incredibly frustrated and we compulsively try to change him or her. Even when we know that our outbursts, criticisms, and advice only make things worse, we are out of control.

There is a profound life lesson hidden in these situations. They provoke a feeling of betrayal and part of this feeling of betrayal has its roots in childhood. But on a deeper level, it brings us face to face with an existential feeling of aloneness that can be hard to bear. We call it the "deprivation meditation." Deprivation is a chronic feeling that something is missing. Out of this feeling that something is missing, we have a compulsive need to resolve our feeling of dissatisfaction and disease. The only way that seems possible is to try to change the other person or the situation that makes us so uncomfortable.

> *The experience of being deprived can be most intense when juxtaposed against an experience of nourishment.*

When we feel loved, and then the love is taken away, it can be devastating. When we have allowed ourselves to open up to someone, to become vulnerable, and then that person leaves, or is not available, it is often felt as an intense betrayal. This feeling of connection, warmth, and love with someone seems like a taste of heaven. Then if that person withdraws his or her love from us, that taste of heaven becomes a taste of hell. That feeling is deprivation.

At the moments when we feel deprived, we normally do not make a connection between our feelings of hurt, irritation, or anger at the other person's behavior to its origin in childhood. We are also not usually aware that in those moments, we are being confronted with existential dis-ease. Instead, we most often feel deep mistrust for the person in our life that has provoked our frustration. We might not show or even be aware of the trigger but may simply pull away from the person and not open ourselves again in a deep way. In any close relationship, we are going to feel deprived and abandoned many times in little and in big ways. It is part of the package but difficult to accept. No one can fill the holes left over from our emotional deprivations in childhood. And no one can shelter us from the existential fact that essentially we are alone and have to face ourselves and death alone.

Yet, it is helpful to understand that by going through the experience of deprivation and by learning to contain the disappointment and frustration of not getting what we want, we build strength inside. This is how we develop real trust and become a whole person. Without it, we never grow up and we stay a child who hopes and expects people and the world to give us what we want. By framing and by understanding deprivation as vital spiritual and emotional experiences, we learn to stay open to what life brings us. We learn that we can welcome any feeling that comes and that gives us tremendous freedom. Instead of pulling away from people and hardening our heart, we develop the space inside to be with the feelings of not getting what we want, even if at times, it feels like we will burn up with frustration.

What is Deprivation?

Usually, there is rarely any doubt what an abandonment experience is. Someone we love leaves us or dies; a lover has an affair or is rarely or never physically or emotionally present. Deprivation can be more subtle. When we are living with someone, our deprivation wound gets triggered in the little ways that the other person does not live up to our expectations. We may feel deprived when the person we are intimate with does or says something that makes us feel separate from him or her. We may feel deprived when a lover or a close friend reveals parts of his or her personality that we don't like—such as being childish and irresponsible or self-centered and inconsiderate. Our deprivation wound can get triggered when we perceive the other person to be dishonest and lacking in integrity, when he or she gets lost in addictive behaviors, or distracts him or herself from facing life. It may even get triggered when he or she smells in a way we don't like, has friends we don't like, or doesn't likes a movie we like.

Deprivation and abandonment trigger the same wound but most of the time, they don't feel the same. When someone leave us or someone close to us dies, most likely, we are plunged directly into the abandonment wound. With deprivation, we are getting small doses of abandonment all the time, yet there is someone there to feel cheated by, to become angry, frustrated, and disappointed with. Our energy can be distracted from feeling the pain of the experience of deprivation and move into blaming the other person for the hurt we feel. Even the smallest thing can be so frustrating and disappointing that we can feel as if we are going to burn up and die of frustration. We easily regress into a child that feels that we should not be treated this way, that it is unfair or unjust that the other person is the way he or she is and if only that person would change a little bit.

At the moment when we feel let down, we usually react in some way—perhaps with blame, anger, revenge, resignation, or withdrawal. Habitually we direct our energy and actions at making the frustration go away. We may cut off from the person, throw a tantrum, leave the relationship, take substances, overeat, or work all the time—anything to feel better.

Buried under our reactions to not getting what we want, lies a space of profound fear.

It is the same fear of separation from love, of never getting what we need, of being forever lonely and unloved, of never being held or supported that we feel when we are abandoned. With deprivation, it comes in smaller doses and more frequently. At these moments, we unknowingly relive earlier experiences that were intolerably painful and frightening. Again, unless we have some understanding for the deeper significance of those moments that provoke this fear, we cannot contain the tremendous fears that arise and be present enough to feel the panic that these situations bring up. We need to see the value of these experiences to be able to contain them and live through them.

Closeness Today Opens Our Buried Feelings of Abandonment

Deprivation, when it occurs in our life today, echoes a deeply buried wound of feeling let down and unloved from past experiences in our childhood. In some way, each one of us felt abandoned early in life—perhaps from a parent leaving the home when we were young, from a parent not being present physically or emotionally, from not being seen, taken in or wanted, from having expectations and demands imposed upon us—there are countless ways that abandonment occurs. The abandonment wound has its roots in the failures of empathy, holding, protection, nurturing, attention, support, and guidance we received as a child. No one has a perfect childhood but even if we did get perfect nurturing, we would still feel an emptiness inside that we must face. The experience of deprivation and abandonment also results from having to leave the womb and later separate from our mother.

As we grow older, we usually bury the pain and fear of these abandonment feelings until we allow ourselves to come close to another person. Then they surface and the abandonment and deprivation appear. When we are facing the frustration and panic of deprivation or the pain of abandonment, it is easy to become lost in bitterness, rage, and despair. Or we move into deep resignation, hold the energy and the rage inside and may even fall into depression.

It is helpful to know that the abandonment/deprivation experience is more than just psychological. It is a profound spiritual rite of passage. It takes us to the deepest place in our soul and opens us up to existence. Certainly the more emotionally deprived we were as children, the harder it is to deal with abandonment and deprivation, but in our experience, no one is spared this terror and this pain. And there is definitely not something wrong with us that we go through this. It is the doorway that we need to go through to connect directly with existence; to feel the trust that arises when we realize that we are held and cared for by existence.

Our Soul Can Realize the Value of Deprivation

While our regressed child desperately and compulsively looks for ways to escape the panic of feeling deprived and abandoned, there is a part of our being inside that attracts it. This part of us knows that learning to feel and contain this fear is a profound rite of passage on our road to recovering our inner sense of self. It is probably the single most significant factor that takes us out of our childish consciousness into maturity.

> *Many relationships become shipwrecked because there is a lack of understanding that if we want to go deep into intimacy with another person in any kind of relationship; we will have to encounter frequent deprivation.*

Anna and Thomas began working with us several years ago. She was in the process of ending a long relationship with her husband with whom she had two children. Thomas is a carefree fellow who had never been in a long-term relationship with anyone. Anna was now convinced that in Thomas she had found the love of her life and panicked whenever he would leave for even a day. She reacted with a mixture of rage and hysterical fear at the slightest indication that Thomas was not totally "there for her." Naturally, this behavior would give him more incentive to leave frequently. Anna did not have the understanding that existence was inviting her to feel her fears and the pain of abandonment. She thought that he was being disrespectful to her for not being more available. After all, he claimed that he loved her and love, in her opinion, meant being present for the other, if not all, then at least most of the time.

Yet in spite of her fears and her reactiveness, she had a strong willingness to understand and feel what was behind all of this. She used our guidance to feel her panic and frustration when he would go away and to find avenues outside the relationship to nourish herself. She trusted our experience and us enough to realize that her pain may have its roots in her past and that there was something important for her to learn. This process took time. In spite of working with her abandoned child and feeling the pain of her childhood experiences, she would still react with rage or hysterics when she felt deprived by Thomas. Yet slowly, she was able to be with the panic without so much reaction. This released a lot of energy in her and she put that energy into starting and running a bed and breakfast hotel. As she was able to contain her fears more, Thomas found that he enjoyed being together with her more. Today, they are doing very well together.

> *As long as we expect another to meet our expectations, we never mature beyond a child who is forever seeking the love he or she did not get.*

As we mature, we begin to accept the other person the way he or she is. We become able to contain the fact of his (or her) being different from us, and maybe even recognize the enrichment of the differences. In isolation, we can avoid confronting the frustration and fear of being deprived and abandoned. But when we allow ourselves to come close to someone, all the longings for intimacy, love, closeness, touch, attention, presence, understanding, and companionship that we have been storing inside begin to come up. The depth of these longings is often unconscious. And with these longings arise fears of not being met when we finally open, of not being listened to, of not being deeply understood, of not having the other person present when we need him or her. Naturally, the more we allow ourselves to open, the more we expect, and the greater the disappointment, pain, frustration, and panic when our expectations are not met. But when we understand that deprivation is part of the package of intimacy, we have one of the most important tools that we need in order to share and sustain love.

Furthermore, we gain a deep sense of empowerment when we learn to contain deprivation. I (Krish) used to have a strong need for approval and respect from a particular friend of mine. It would drive me nuts. I was unable to relate to him in a natural way because I always wanted something from him that I felt he didn't give me. The more I wanted, the more frustrated I felt. But over time, I got the point. The approval I wanted from him (as with my older brother as a child) was never going to come from him. When I finally stopped seeking it, something matured inside and paradoxically, our relationship became real.

A Conscious Decision to Go In and Feel

Because we have two sides of us—our regressed child who wants to run away from discomfort and pain and our soul that recognizes the value of pain and frustration—it is important to make a conscious choice to go in and feel rather than habitually react or try to distract ourselves from feeling.

A woman in one of our seminars was very upset with her boyfriend because she felt that he was not present. She complained that he was always "in his head—like a computer," that he was busy doing other things rather than relate to her, and that he was not willing to feel her feelings or even his feelings. She was preoccupied with whether or not to leave him and kept going back and forth between ending the relationship and then coming back to him and hoping that he would change and be more open to her. Finally, they both came to a seminar hoping that this would resolve their problems.

As is usually the case, the deprivation that she was experiencing today was merely a reflection of an earlier childhood experience. This woman's father was distant and unavailable to her and this generated a deep hunger to have a man present and attentive to her emotionally. And, as often happens, the deprivation wound is combined with shame, which shows itself as us not feeling worthy of receiving the attention and love She felt that she really did not deserve to have a man be there for her. Projecting her pain on her husband and making him responsible for it was a distraction.

When we let go of wanting the other to be different, it forces us to face the fear that we will feel deprived forever. At first, we often resist this life lesson because we may have a strong belief that by letting go and accepting the deprivation, we will never get what we need. We might have learned from experiences that the only way to get what we need is by fighting for it. It is important to have deep patience and compassion for ourselves when recovering from a loss or rejection or when coming to terms with how another person is not giving us what we want.

There is no way to "play it right." We will probably react in some way toward the other. We may run to some kind of addictive behavior to ease the pain, we may find ourselves trapped in compulsive behavior like calling the person or trying to convince him or her that we have changed, or to take us back or to explain why he or she left. Finally, we may find ourselves obsessively thinking the same thoughts repeatedly without any way to stop them. To face and be present to these feelings can be so frightening because we literally feel that we are going to die. We can feel so restless and agitated that we feel like a hamster in a wheel. Or so depressed and full of despair that it takes every effort just to get up in the morning. Our mind is racing and nothing seems to help or to take away the panic.

Part of the difficulty of abandonment and deprivation is that it is intimately connected with our shame and it is hard to separate the two.

> *When we are left, when someone disappoints us, or when someone pulls away emotionally, not only do we have to deal with the loneliness; we also have to feel the shame of feeling not worthy of love.*

Most of the time, we have a voice inside that tells us we are not worthy of having someone truly present, loving, accepting, and caring for us. Someone who did not feel taken in as a child does not feel worthy of being taken in as an adult. In the grips of our pain, it is hard to tell which is worse—the loneliness and fear that we will be alone forever or the shame of feeling unlovable. Therefore, these times of abandonment and deprivation are like a shame and abandonment cocktail.

Dealing with Times of Deprivation and Abandonment

It's our experience that the greatest hurdle in recovering from the experiences of abandonment and deprivation is not the pain and sorrow, but the fear and the fighting with the pain. Inside each of us is an endless reservoir to deal with loss and frustration. But it is difficult when we do not understand what is happening and why it is happening. This lack of understanding and awareness causes fear. And on top of that we were never taught that pain has any value. We never learned that pain helps us to mature. So instead of allowing the pain we usually fight it. And by fighting, it becomes suffering and lingers on much longer than if it was accepted and felt and allowed to move through us.

> *Once we stop resisting and take these painful experiences as unavoidable journeys into the soul, something settles deep inside.*

Love brings loss; it is part of the experience of love. If we open our heart, our heart will hurt many times. As we become closer to someone, our deprivation experiences can often become more intense and more frequent. Deprivation and abandonment experiences open hidden places in the unconsciousness that cannot heal unless they are opened and felt. The terror and pain of the abandonments we experienced as a child lay dormant inside and often only get triggered with similar experiences today.

If we allow the feelings of fear and pain without resistance, they pass. Then the confusion and shock, the rage and resentment and finally the sorrow and grief fall into place. When we embrace deprivation and abandonment, we open to a profound peacefulness inside. Most of our fight with life is precisely because we resist feeling our helplessness and our aloneness.

Letting Go of Wanting Things to Change

We have been working with a woman for quite a few years whose story with men has been a string of heartaches. She is attracted to men who are not willing to commit to being totally with her and these men generally end up having affairs with other women. She is a very intelligent, vivacious, and inspiring person, but when she is around a man, she loses herself and becomes submissive, compliant, and collapsed. When she is in a relationship, she complains that her man is not available enough, when she is out of a relationship; she complains that she cannot find the man she is looking for. She has worked with herself for many years and knows about abandonment and shame. She recognizes that she is attracting unavailable men because of her shame; her hunger and desperation to be in a relationship pushes them away.

As she grows older, she becomes increasingly desperate that she will never find the man she wants. She also feels desperate because all the inner work she has done has not changed her patterns. Two years ago, she met a man and they have been together since. I have spoken to her regularly over this time and have asked her in detail, if she notices that she is relating differently with him than with men in her past. She says, and we feel it is true, that something has profoundly changed. She feels herself, honors herself, and she is not losing her dignity or integrity with him. Her story is truly an example that if we are committed enough to working through our wounds and our dysfunction, we will learn what we need to learn.

It is natural that there comes a time when we wonder how long we have to keep feeling abandoned, deprived, and full of shame. We wonder when or if things are going to change. This is one of the most frequent questions that arise in our work, particularly with people who have extensively explored their wounds. At times, it can seem brutally unfair that our lives and our relationships are not working in spite of our sincerity and commitment to the inner work.

We often ask people to work with two questions:

1. *"Am I still hoping that someone will rescue me from feeling my fears, pain, and loneliness?"*

2. *"Do I feel worthy of having someone love me and be present for me?"*

Most often, the answers to these questions are yes and no, respectively. In some ways, the most profound aspect of working with abandonment, deprivation, and shame is recognizing how much our thoughts and behaviors are still in the grips of our regressed child who wants to be rescued and who feels unworthy of love.

> *When we appreciate and accept what we are getting, we get what we want.*

It is a strange paradox that when we are able to relax and deeply accept the experiences that life brings us, we are fulfilled, and then even our deepest desires get fulfilled. Once we deeply accept that shame and aloneness are not going to go away, once we settle into them without fighting, something transforms. Then the pattern of our relating changes.

* * *

CHAPTER 10:

LEARNING THE TWO LESSONS –

When to Set a Limit and When to Contain Frustration

I teach a different kind of love.
It does not end in friendship but begins in friendship.
It begins in silence, in awareness.
It is a love which is your own creation, which is not blind.
Such a love can last forever and can grow deeper and deeper.
Don't let biology dominate you.
Your consciousness should be your master.
Osho

In chapter 8, we explored what helps us to feel empowered and how to learn to respond to invasions. In the previous chapter, we explored the issue of abandonment and deprivation. These two situations confront us with our deepest and most primal fears—the fear of being invaded and abused and the fear of being unloved and rejected. Regardless of whether we are being invaded and disrespected or deprived of someone's love and attention, it brings up the same feelings of betrayal. It brings up the same feelings of rage, frustration, resignation, and even hopelessness. But in terms of our inner growth, these two situations are profoundly different. The spiritual lessons that they are teaching us are different. And they confront us with the need to respond in radically different ways.

We have been working with a woman who is married and has an eighteen-month-old child with a man she has been with for five years. She is distraught because her man drinks and does drugs, relies on her financially, and often does not live up to his agreement to take care of their son while she is working. She loves him and understands that his difficulties and addictions have their roots in a troubled childhood but she feels overburdened in caring for their child and resentful that he is so irresponsible.

Is this a case of containment or setting limits?

What she has learned through her work with us is that often she excuses and minimizes his irresponsibility by "understanding" his troubles. She sees that it is hard for her to state clearly what she needs and what is not OK for her about his behavior and then she either gives up or explodes. In all of her relationships with men, she has put her own needs aside and focused on taking care and sacrificing herself. This behavior is fueled by a deep shame that she is not worthy of having a man who is there for her and who respects her. Slowly she is learning to say what she needs and is beginning to feel that she deserves someone who can step up to the plate. But the deeper issue for her has been to accept that her partner is not motivated to go into recovery for his addictions and become responsible and accountable in his life. We have explained to her that a person is either in addiction or in recovery; there is no middle ground. But in her fears of losing him and breaking up the family, she has allowed herself to be manipulated over and over again by his promises and his excuses. Finally, she has been able to see that he is not going to change and she cannot hold out any longer. With that clarity, she found the strength to accept that the relationship cannot continue; she is ready to feel the pain of the loss. Her process has been an opportunity to learn both lessons—how to set limits and how to contain pain.

> *When we are experiencing an invasion or disrespect, it is not appropriate to simply be with the frustration and contain the feelings. It is a situation that gives us an opportunity to respond in a new way, perhaps by setting a limit.*

In the example in chapter 8 of the woman who is being invaded and disrespected by her husband when they make love, it is a lesson for her to stand up for herself and not permit this kind of disrespect. It is not a time to be overrun and imagine that all she needs to do is forgive or pretend that what is happening does not matter to her. The challenge for her is to face her fears of saying no, to learn to be clearer about what she wants and needs, and to be able to communicate this with her husband.

However, in the example of the woman who complained that her boyfriend always had his head in the computer—complaining or making demands on him is not creative for her. Her challenge is to learn to contain her frustration of his being the way he is. Her challenge is to face the abandonment wound that gets triggered when he is not available to her.

Sometimes the Distinction Is Not So Clear

Life invites us to make the distinction between these two situations in order that we can learn to respond in a way that brings us more dignity, self-respect and self-love. But sometimes it is not so clear which lesson the life situation we are faced with invites us to learn. Often a given situation combines both lessons. For instance, Marie gets enraged with her boyfriend when she asks him a question and he doesn't answer. She asks again until finally she gets his attention by screaming at him or leaving the room in a rage. What is her lesson in this situation? Is he abusing her by not answering and does she need to set a limit about his ignoring her? Or does she need to contain her frustration that he is not available? In this situation, existence is inviting Marie to respect herself by expressing that it is important for her that he answers her. This is an important step of validating her feelings and needs. At the same time, she needs to learn to contain the frustration when he is not answering her, as he may not change even after she expresses her needs.

Martina feels disturbed when Hans, her husband, spends time doing "his own things." When he is working at the computer or going out with friends, she hounds him to tell her how long he will be working or how long he will be away. He is disturbed by her insisting and is afraid that he will be punished each time he spends time with himself or with others away from her. Because of his fear, he feels guilty each time he leaves and when he comes back, he is ambivalent and not present. This ambivalence and lack of presence enrages her even more because she feels invaded and abused. By being with Hans, Martina is learning to contain her frustration of his not being there and feel her abandonment each time he separates. At the same time, she also needs to say something when he comes to her out of guilt and is not present. Hans is learning to face his fears of separating, and give himself the right to take his space and set limits to her attempts of controlling him. But he is also being tested to contain and feel his panic that she will take revenge and punish him.

When we are teaching these two lessons, people often present us with situations in which their lovers are making love with someone else. They want to know which lesson this presents—invasion or deprivation. We will take up this question in more detail in a later chapter but basically, we are each free to live our life as we wish to. It is not an invasion if our lover chooses to sleep with another person. It opens our abandonment wound and we need to be with the pain of that.

It is a different story if he or she is not honest. For instance, if you suspect that your lover is having an affair and inquire, and he or she denies it, this is clearly a gross invasion if, in fact, it is true. On a more subtle level, we consider it an invasion if one lover is having an affair and hides it even if he or she is not asked. The reason is that whether we realize it or not, somewhere deep inside, we know or at least suspect anyway. Emotionally, we become a hostage of the other person's dishonesty. But if the situation is out in the open, even if we are willing to be with the pain that this causes, there may come a time, after having been with the pain, when we get clear that we do not want to accept being with someone who is sleeping with another person. Out of love and respect for ourselves, we may need to move on. At a certain point, being with the pain of the abandonment can become self-destructive.

Focusing on the Inner Knowing

In these two life lessons, there is a natural way that our life energy wants to move and if we listen, it becomes clear. In the first case, our life energy moves toward affirming our dignity and self-respect and not compromising. In the second case, our life energy will naturally move toward more maturity as we learn to contain pain and accept our aloneness, accepting the person or the situation as it is.

> *Our intuition naturally moves us toward integrity even if it means having to say no to someone.*
> *Our intuition also naturally moves to find the space to let the other person be who he or she is even if it frustrates us.*

Out of fear, we may not follow the voice or feeling of our intuition; nevertheless, it is there and we know it. It also knows that deep down we are alone even though we may be resisting this fact by blaming the outside when we are not getting what we want. When we follow our natural inner knowing rather than reacting from our wounded child who is frightened or hurt, we feel a deep sense of integrity and dignity. And every little step we take in this direction releases tremendous energy that then helps us move on.

When we cannot set a limit or affirm our needs, a child overtakes us who is afraid of punishment or feels that he or she has no right to say no. When we panic and cannot contain our frustration when someone is not giving us what we feel we need, our fears of abandonment overwhelm us. These fears are very strong. But the force and power of our inner knowing is stronger.

It can help to recognize that it serves a higher spiritual purpose both for ourselves and for the other person when we follow our intuition. In our relating situations, we are inviting opportunities to learn these two lessons. They are profound life lessons which intuitively, we want to learn. Intuitively, we also know that it is much more loving to contain our frustration and panic rather than trying to control the other person. It is also much more loving to ourselves and to the other person to be clear about our limits and to affirm them. When we affirm our integrity, the other person gets a clear message, knows where we are and can trust us.

> *When we are triggered by feeling disrespected or by being deprived, it is natural, human, and predictable that we get taken over by our emotional child and react in habitual ways. But with more precise awareness, we begin to realize that we are not only this emotional child. We do have a choice. We may continue to react but at any time, we can wake up from the automatic reaction and follow our natural wisdom.*

Exercise:

Bring to mind the last time you felt frustrated or disappointed by someone close and important to you.

Ask yourself:

1. *Was this a direct invasion and disrespect to my being or was I just not having my expectations met?*

2. *What was my reaction?*

3. *Did that reaction bring me more or less dignity?*

(If we respond to an invasion by setting a limit, or if we respond to a deprivation and unmet expectation by going in and feeling it, we feel more dignity.)

* * *

CHAPTER 11:

LEARNING RESPONSIBILITY –

Discarding Duty for Honesty and Integrity

Move, but don't move the way fear moves you.
Rumi

The word "responsibility" can have some ugly connotations. It can suggest "duty" or "rules" that many of us had mindlessly imposed upon us and we followed or still follow because we have been told that this is the "right" and "proper" way to live. Authentic responsibility means being aware of the impact of our actions and being willing to feel how our behavior affects others. Responsibility means "response-ability"—the ability to be present to each moment and respond appropriately to each situation we are confronted with. When we are accountable in this way, not only can others trust us but, even deeper, we respect and trust ourselves.

The Price of Our Irresponsibility

In a recent seminar, there was a participant, (we will call her Sandra), who did not want to do her share of the small work chores which each person was invited to do. In some of the seminar places we work, especially those that are also a community for permanent residents, we ask people to help keep the environment clean during the workshop. It is not a requirement but if someone does not feel able to do a chore, he or she is asked to inform the organizer and a replacement will be found. In this case, Sandra did not do the work but also did not bother to tell anyone. The person she was supposed to be working with felt disrespected and angry because she was left to do her chore alone.

When she brought it up in the group that she felt disrespected, Sandra defended herself and would not acknowledge that she had done anything disrespectful. She felt that it was her freedom to do what she wanted, and her freedom not to have to explain why she did what she did. The group supported the woman who felt disrespected and pointed out to her that it would have been fine for her not to do the chore as long as she informed her partner. Sandra felt alienated from the group and went deeper into her familiar feelings of mistrust and isolation, which was how she lived much of her life.

> *When we are not taking responsibility for our actions, we become alienated and isolated and we often blame others for closing off to us. Furthermore, when we are unaccountable, the price we pay is that we are seen and treated as a child; deep inside, we feel like one as well.*

As a child, I (Krish) was known in my family as a lovable fuckup. My older brother was the proficient one, and I was the one who could not really be counted on. I covered my insecurity by half purposely making mistakes at things I did and pretending to know things. My brother used to call me "the great source of misinformation." It was a painful vicious cycle. My behavior deepened my negative identity and the deeper the identity, the more compulsive the behavior became. I blamed others for not seeing me as grown-up but how could I expect others to treat me as an adult when I was not behaving like one?

Later, when I entered into therapy, I recognized the roots of this identity—I never felt that I could keep up with my older brother who excelled at everything he did so I did the opposite. Since it seemed to me that I couldn't compete with my brother for my parents by excelling, I chose another route, which was to be a clown. It also helped to lessen the pressures and expectations to be as good as he was. Slowly, painstakingly, by facing my fears and understanding the origin of all of this, and taking risks to discover and nourish my gifts, I worked through this identity.

One man was sharing with us that his wife had recently slept with his best friend. When we dug a little deeper into his story, it turned out that he had had a child with his wife but at the time of the pregnancy, she did not feel she had the time to have a child because she was both working full time and learning a new career. He pleaded with her and offered to do the major part of the mothering while she was studying because she was so busy. They had the baby.

Now, three years later, he is resentful, moody, collapsed, and angry inside. He blames her for not being able to do what he wants to do. For him, having a child with her was more of a romantic fantasy than a reality and now he does not want to face the reality of having to take care of the child. Furthermore, he has not been willing to take the steps to create a life for himself, using as an excuse that he has to take care of their child. She is still in love with him but feels deeply betrayed. She acted out this betrayal and rage by sleeping with his best friend.

> *Often, becoming aware of our unaccountability is the first step toward becoming accountable.*

Being Irresponsible with Our Energy

Responsibility and accountability do not only concern fulfilling a commitment or a promise. It also concerns how we handle our emotions and our energy. In a recent workshop, one of the men shared frequently during the periods of open work but when he was not speaking and did not have the attention of the group, he would not listen to others and sometimes, he would even lie down and appear to be sleeping. When one of the other participants told him that he felt disrespected by this behavior, he became angry and defensive, claiming that he was listening. But it was clear to others that when he was not the center of attention, he lost interest. Later in the workshop, his wife shared with us that he had beaten her recently and she was afraid of his violence both for herself and for her infant child. During the course of the nine-day workshop, many of the participants became intimidated by him and this allowed him to feel a certain control and power in the group. But what he gained in power and control, he lost in warmth and affection from the others.

Blame

Another way we are irresponsible with our energy is when we blame other people, the environment, or circumstances for the way we feel. We make the outside responsible for our inner state of being. Perhaps we learned this form of relating to life and other people from our parents and blame becomes automatic. My father (Amana) would constantly blame someone for his "bad luck" and could go on and on about how horrible people were. He primarily targeted my mother's parents, whom he felt disrespected by, but he also found any reason for blaming anyone. He became more and more bitter, letting his own inability to take responsibility for his life take over, drowning his disappointment in alcohol, abusing his body in every possible way, and eventually giving up on life when we was just thirty-eight years old.

The shadow of his behavior has been with me my whole life. I learned early on that this is the way to deal with life when it is not giving you what you want—either blame someone or give up. I countered this infection from my father by learning to become highly responsible. Yet at times, I get sucked into my father's depressive vortex. I can literally feel it as an energy phenomenon taking over, especially when I am tired and exhausted. There are moments when I feel unable to give to myself what I need and at the same time feel unable to ask for support. It is a space of utter darkness and helplessness and requires all my strength to watch it, to go for a walk, or to sit quietly and feel it. It helps to know where it comes from and to understand that in this giving up I bond with my father—a deep childlike longing to be with him. When I realize that, I can take the time to give to myself what I really need instead of giving into depression.

Anger

We are often irresponsible with our anger. Most of us carry much unexplored and unconscious rage inside and when we don't work with it in a healthy way, it comes out in inappropriate ways.

We worked with a couple who initially appeared to be having a loving and intimate relationship. We learned later that for a long time, the man had been having unpredictable explosions of rage, often when he had something to drink. In those moments, he would be verbally abusive with his wife and even humiliate her in front of their children. Even though he is now working with himself and has begun to be more responsible with his rage, his wife had developed so much mistrust that she felt she could not open to him. He now acknowledges his abusiveness to her but still is not willing to feel the pain that he has caused her. Until he opens his heart to feeling the pain he has caused her, she will not be able to open and trust him.

Another common way of dealing irresponsibly with our anger and hurt is to express them indirectly by cutting off and withholding our love and our energy. Although this is a very common way of dealing with hurt, it is dysfunctional because it is indirect. The energy stays locked in our system and poisons us—our withholding behavior can last for years without our having penetrated deeper into our feelings. A man in one of our workshops did not admit that he was angry with his wife for not wanting to make love to him when he wanted. His reaction to this rejection was to become moody and walk around the house feeling irritated and grumpy. When she would ask him if something was wrong, he would say that he was not feeling well. His repression of his anger went underground and from there created all kinds of symptoms in his body that eventually led to a deep depression.

Our Body

Another very important aspect of growing up is taking responsibility for our body. We become responsible for our body when we begin to feel it from the inside. That teaches us to give our body what it needs in terms of food, sleep, environments, and exercise. By mistreating our bodies with unhealthy addictions or simply not listening to its needs, we remain regressed and reinforce our poor self-esteem. It becomes a painful cycle because we judge ourselves and then become more self-destructive. A child has no sense for what is healthy and what feels right in the body. He or she simply wants instant gratification and does not think of the consequences. As we learn to take more responsibility, we become a parent to ourselves and treat our body in a life-positive way. The situation becomes more complicated when we know that we are being self-destructive but feel unable to make the necessary changes. Then our responsibility is to reach out for the help and support we need to change those life negative patterns.

As a child, I (Amana) had become very alienated and cut off from my body. I grew up in an environment in which everyone focused on external things and I witnessed people around me relating in ways that were painful and superficial. At the same time, it was threatening to feel anything, as feelings were considered abnormal. As a result, I stopped feeling my body and as a teenager began mistreating myself with cigarettes, drugs, depriving myself of sleep, and eating junk food. Then I would diet to lose weight and obsess about calories.

In my early twenties, when I started therapy groups and meditation, I began for the first time to get an inner feeling for my body and for what my body would like—what it would like to eat and how it wanted to move. I learned to listen moment to moment to the feelings in the body and to respect that. I began taking walks in nature, dancing, running, and practicing yoga. Now, I weigh the same that I did as a teenager but I have never dieted since and am no longer concerned about calories. I eat what I feel like eating and my body has come in tune with itself without any struggle.

Money and the Material World

Another of our challenges is to learn to be responsible in the area of money and the material world. In this arena, we can be sloppy and unaccountable in many ways – not paying back debts, borrowing something and not returning it, not taking care of bills, building up credit cards debts, not taking care of practical details such as insurance or taxes, allowing another person to regularly pay for us and so on. In this area, it is important to see if our regressed child is in control. For example, we have an acquaintance that regularly does not share expenses at restaurants or in taxis, claiming that she doesn't have change or will pay later, but then she conveniently forgets. We have another friend who leaves unopened bills on his desk, builds up huge credit card debts and then declares bankruptcy. Or another friend who regularly borrows items but has to be reminded to return them. I (Krish) have at different times in my life been guilty of all of these behaviors. Unless we confront our fears of dealing with the material world and our unconscious desire to be taken care of, our regressed child takes over in this area. It is a common expression of fear but when we behave this way, we pay a high price. We lose self-respect.

Another way our regressed child can be in control in this area is by obsessing about making money and accumulating large sums of money. It may not look like the regressed child, but our regressed child drives anything that is compulsive and automatic. In this case, we may not be responsibly dealing with all aspects of our life but focusing too much attention on money.

The Ingredients of Learning Responsibility

In our experience, there are three aspects to working through our irresponsibility and unaccountability. The first is to understand and feel how it is connected to our original wounds of betrayal and invasion. This is the root. The second is to be willing to feel the way this behavior affects others and to feel the pain that it causes. The third is a sincere heartfelt soul desire to grow up.

1. Feeling the Fear behind Our Irresponsibility and Dishonesty

We don't become responsible simply by deciding to be more responsible. The process is deeper than that. We have to start by going to the roots and exploring where this irresponsibility and lack of integrity comes from. When someone calls attention to our irresponsible and unaccountable behavior or if we become aware of it ourselves, normally we deal with it by either becoming defensive or feeling apologetic and guilty. Neither of which is very helpful. It is certainly healthier to recognize our lack of responsibility and feel guilty about it rather than to deny and defend it, but guilt alone does not transform anything. It is a good first step but only a first step.

We don't normally take the time to connect our unaccountable or irresponsible behavior to our wounds. But actually, the source of this behavior is our trauma and the shame and shock we carry inside. Sandra (who didn't want to do the chore or ask someone else to do it) had become numb with shock from being raised by a mother who had unpredictable fits of rage and who left her family periodically and did not return for months at a time. She was not aware of how deeply traumatized she was but the result of this trauma was that she had become desensitized to herself and to others. She had learned to survive by being indifferent to others and to how her behavior affected others. In this way she could stay safe and protected in her isolation. For her to apologize would make her vulnerable (to the attacks of her mother) and that would be like facing death and total destruction.

Most often, we behave irresponsibly because there is so much fear inside and our self-image is already so damaged that we do not know what it would be like to be responsible and accountable. One of the owners of a seminar house where we work has a habit of making lavish promises but has difficulty following through with them. He has tremendous pressure inside to get approval from authority figures like us and this pressure causes him to make grandiose offers. This kind of grandiosity is a common way that our unaccountability covers our fears. Our fear drives us to become habitually dishonest. Our imprinting and our conditioning is to be dishonest even if verbally, we may have been told to be honest. It is terrifying to be honest. We risk rejection, disapproval, rage, humiliation, or loss.

I (Krish) have exaggerated to enhance my image, told half-truths to protect myself, and lied to get what I wanted often without even noticing that I was being dishonest. Outright dishonesty, exaggeration, and half-truths have not only been a part of my behavior as long as I can remember but also a deeply imbedded part of my self-image. For me to begin altering this habitual behavior was an ongoing process of noticing when these situations arise and confronting the fear behind it.

Often we are dishonest for fear of hurting someone. We seldom realize that our dishonesty usually is more hurtful than if we came out directly with our thoughts or our feelings. We may also be deeply afraid of the consequences—anger or rejection—if we were to become honest, especially if we have something to hide. The closer we come to someone, the higher the standard of honesty becomes if we want to maintain and deepen intimacy.

Recently we worked with a woman who was having difficulty in her relationships with men. Although she was in a new relationship, she was still longing after a man whom she had met seventeen years earlier, who lived on another continent, and now was married to someone else. She felt that the new relationship was good but she was not attracted to him and she did not enjoy making love with him. When we asked her what it was about her new man that she did not find attractive, she said that he did not look like her old boyfriend and she judged him for having sexual problems. We asked her if she had been honest with him about her judgments and her comparisons to her other friend.

She said that she could not imagine saying such things to him because it would hurt him too much. She never considered that intimacy is based on honesty. She had never been truly honest with people in her life because no one had ever been honest with her. We suggested to her that her lack of attraction to him was probably more hurtful than being honest and that most certainly, he already felt her judgments anyway. This was a revelation to her. In her case, being honest would mean not only sharing her judgments of her new lover, but also sharing her fears and her insecurity. Very often, we create excuses not to open to someone, as it is too frightening. The mind creates a smoke screen that the reason we are not open is the person, or it compares that person with a former lover. All just an attempt to not feel the fear of opening and being here and now.

> *To love and trust each other, we have to be willing to be honest. By honesty, we mean that we need to share anything which if not exposed would create distance and mistrust between us and the other person. Honesty is probably the*

last thing we want to be accountable for and it's hard to recognize the price we pay for being dishonest.

At the core of our lack of responsibility and accountability is a fear to grow up and be present to the moment. For many of us, the prospect of learning to "grow up and be responsible" seems very unattractive because, as a child, we witnessed people becoming repressed, unhappy, and burdened with their "responsibility." With that kind of conditioning, a strong force inside of us may not want to grow up. It seems dull, dead, serious, and much too much work. We may become rebellious in reaction to this repressive conditioning but lack of accountability and responsibility can become a part of our rebellion. And this can become a way of avoiding our deeper fears of facing the practical details and responsibilities of daily life.

I (Krish) rebelled strongly against the ideas of "responsibility" that I was taught. A big part of that rebellion was rejecting many aspects of the conventional world. For years, the last thing I wanted to do was become burdened with a family, conventional job, house, mortgage, insurances, and so on. I sincerely believed that as a spiritual seeker living in spiritual communes, I was rejecting all of that. But times changed. There came a time when I recognized that it was also part of my growth and maturity to confront the practicalities of living in the world.

When I left the commune that I had been living in for many years and finally bought a house, got insurances, etc., I had to make a supreme effort not to allow my fears to take over and let things slide. I could not believe how many details needed attending to and often find myself wondering if becoming so encumbered with practical details is worth it. But it seems important, maturing, and creative to deal with the fears of "being in the world." (It certainly pleased my parents when I made this step but fortunately, I did not do it for that reason.) I had experienced how it was to live differently. I was able to make a choice to re-enter the world. My mother calls it becoming a "mensch," which in Yiddish means "a responsible man."

2. *Feeling the Effect of Our Irresponsibility*

The second aspect of learning responsibility and accountability is to be willing to feel what it is like for others when we behave in a way that is disrespectful, inconsiderate, or hurtful to another person and to feel how this kind of behavior affects our life.

In one of our workshops, we do an exercise that includes handing out a list of the common ways in which we were invaded as a child and perhaps continue to be invaded today. The purpose of the exercise is to give people a deeper understanding of what constitutes invasion. We tell people that our focus is not on how we invade others but on how we were and continue to get invaded because, once we have deeply felt our own trauma, it is much more difficult to continue to be insensitive to others. But invariably, people recognize how they invade others and start to feel guilty. Guilt alone does not help because feeling guilty is often a shortcut for not having to feel the pain of how our unconsciousness has hurt someone. Real transformation can happen only when we are willing to open up to feeling the impact, the effect of our actions. When we are willing to feel the pain we are causing another person, we are not able to continue doing it.

For this process to be transformative, we have to reach the point where we actually take in the person who has received our irresponsibility and unaccountability and feel what it would be like to be him or her. We have to take them into our heart and feel as they feel. But we are not able to take in another person's pain until we have taken in our own. The process starts with us. We invade because we were invaded and feeling the pain of having been invaded paves the way for deeper sensitivity in our relationships. By taking in our own pain, feeling the pain in our body, we create the inner space to take in the pain of another. In the example of Sandra, the reason she was so unaware of others was simply because she was unaware of herself and her own hurt and pain.

3. The Decision to Grow Up

When we deeply feel the effect of our irresponsibility something inside matures. It is an inner decision to grow up and take responsibility for our own life; realizing the freedom it brings to be responsible. Through this maturing our shame and shock begins to heal and our shamed self-image starts changing. When we have become used to a certain self-image that is shame-based and involves a history of behaving in irresponsible and unaccountable ways, we don't know anything else. Our behavior is automatic and so deeply conditioned that we are not even aware of it.

> *We start to change by beginning to take small steps toward living in a way that is dignified and honest. It is in our hands to create our life exactly the way we would like it. We are not a victim of circumstances. We play a very important part in how our life forms itself.*

Exercise:

Ask yourself:

1. *Where in my life am I acting irresponsibly and without accountability? In work, relating, health, something with money, or my body?*

2. *In what ways am I acting irresponsibly or without accountability?*

3. *If I explore my insecurities and fears, what is the reason I am acting this way?*

4. *What small steps could and would I be willing to make to bring myself more dignity and self-respect?*

* * *

CHAPTER 12:

LESSONS IN LOVING –

What Creates Trust between Lovers and Friends

There are thousands of people who have been so wounded by
human relationship,
They have dropped out of all human love.
To be in love with a human being is not an easy affair.
Love needs a clarity of vision.
Love is a new phenomenon that has arisen in
human consciousness.
You will have to learn it.
Osho

So far, we have been discussing what we consider the basics of real trustfulness. We have said that trust begins by learning to trust ourselves—our feelings, our intuition, and our body signals. We have also stressed that to learn trust, we need to grow up and choose not to be run by our regressed child inside. Now it's time to look at trust between lovers and friends. In this chapter, we would like to share with you some keys that we have found to be extremely helpful for keeping love alive and deepening. We call it, "learning to stay in the love current."

Living together with another person is quite an adventure. It is certainly a challenge and an enormous accomplishment for two people to learn to live together in a flow that continues day after day, year after year, enjoying each other and deepening in love and trust. Often what happens is just the opposite, a couple becomes bored, unappreciative, resentful, or ungrateful. Even though along the way, we have had to deal with conflicts and misunderstandings and some of them have been strong, we have been able to move through without holding on to resentments or pulling away from each other energetically because of lingering unresolved feelings.

Every time we move through a conflict, we come out of the situation with more love and more understanding for the mystery of love and the mystery of the other person. Every conflict is an opportunity to learn more about the other person and ourselves even though when we go through it, it may feel like having entered hell. Neither of us imagined before that this kind of relating was possible and that it was possible to move through conflicts together when our primal wounds get triggered and the other person seems like the enemy. In fact, this is one of the reasons that motivated us to write this book.

Six Keys

Trust that develops between two people is not a mystery. It is based on certain understandings.

> *1. For trust to grow between lovers, it is essential that we start to recognize and take responsibility for when our behavior is taken over by our regressed child.*

We can recognize our regressed child when we feel emotional and when our behavior is charged with emotion. We can also recognize our regressed child when we are either seeking to be rescued or when we are rescuing another. Or it may show itself in our addictions; either to substances like food, cigarettes, or drugs or to some activity like sex, entertainment, shopping, working, and so on.

>*2. For love and trust to grow, we need to get clear about our priorities whether we want to focus our energy with one person or have many lovers. We can have depth or diversity but not both at the same time and it is our responsibility to feel what we want and need and communicate that clearly.*

If we are having many love affairs, trust does not grow. It takes time for trust to develop. It is like a delicate flower that needs time and nourishment to grow.

>*3. For trust to build, we have to honor ourselves and not give ourselves away for "love." In short, we cannot compromise by giving up vital aspects of our life and life energy that are important for our fulfillment just for the sake of the relationship.*

This means that we need to follow our energy even if at times it separates us from our lover. It may mean to continue a hobby, a sport, pursuing a spiritual path, seeing friends, and so on, even if this doesn't involve our partner or even if our partner gets threatened by this. We may also need to say "no" to someone if his or her needs conflict with our own.

>*4. In order for two people to be able to trust and go deeper with each other, there must be an ongoing commitment to open to one another. A part of this commitment is a willingness to spend time together to nourish the relation-*

*ship, to bring awareness to power games and
to become aware of our wounds.*

Our defenses are deeply ingrained and usually highly robotic and
unconscious. So, it takes some effort to consciously drop our protections and our isolation and allow the other person in. Another
aspect of this point is that we have to be willing to take an honest look at our power games and strategies and be willing to drop
them and become vulnerable. To allow the relating to mature it is
important to recognize that it takes time spent together for this
to happen. It doesn't happen by two people living together but
remaining energetically separate.

> *5. For love and trust to deepen, we need to
> take responsibility for our own spiritual and cre-
> ative fulfillment rather than use the relationship
> as our sole and major source of nourishment.*

It destroys the relating if we put all our focus on the other person,
expecting him or her to bring us the fulfillment that we have not
found in ourselves.

> *6. For love and trust to deepen, we have to
> be willing to face our own inner emptiness and
> loneliness.*

It destroys trust if we use the relationship to run away from our
fears of loneliness by clinging to the other or expecting him or her
to shelter us from our emptiness.

We would like to elaborate on each of these six keys.

Key #1 – Recognizing When We Relate from Our Regressed Child

When our relating is filled with reaction, criticism, drama, expectations, demands, blame, or trying to change, analyze, or fix the
other person, it is a sign that our regressed child is in command. The

darker aspect of this energy is revenge, manipulation, withholding, attacking, and judging the other person to get what we want or because we are not getting what we want. When the regressed child has taken over and there is no awareness about this, both people in the relationship will develop deeper and deeper mistrust for each other as time goes on. Some popular movies, such as *Who's Afraid of Virginia Wolfe* and *Bitter Moon*, have demonstrated this very vividly. In both cases, the characters were unknowingly possessed by the consciousness of their regressed children. One of the supreme challenges of intimate relating is that it provokes our regressed child to come to the surface no matter how hard we try to suppress it. And usually, unconsciously we pick a person to be with who most intensely provokes our regressed child.

Linda is a client of ours who was recently left by a man that she had been with for over four years. During their time together, their sexual attraction for each other was very strong and in some way formed the basis of their relating. He never really took her in as a person or as a woman. He was not yet healed enough from his own wounds to take a woman in and he kept the relating mostly on the level of power games and control. (With him in control.) As a result, she always felt insecure and unappreciated. She was never sure when he would leave her for another woman and always anticipated the worst. This situation was a painful re-enactment of her shame of never feeling attractive enough for a "real man." This had its roots in her relationship with her rejecting father. In her relationship, as in her previous ones, she was still looking for a man to give her the feeling that she is deeply loved for who she is because inside she feels unlovable and unworthy.

These covert demands eventually pushed her lover away. He wanted a woman and not a little girl looking for a father. Now that the relationship is over, she can see things that she could not see before. By working intensely with herself, she can see how in her shame, she was drawn to a man who in some way rejected her from the start. She can also see that she was projecting unrealistic demands on him—the hidden desire that he take care of her. At first, the pain of the rejection and the separation was very strong. She was immersed in her shame and feelings of abandonment. But with time, she is gaining confidence and strength in a way which she has not experienced before.

This example illustrates some of the most common ways that relating from our regressed child sabotages the relationship. The game we often play when we are lost in our regressed child is: "I need you and you need to take care of me." And from the other side (and it always takes two), "You need me and I can't let you down." Linda was still clinging to the fantasy that she could find validation and protection from her lover. He was hiding in old defensive patterns of being a rescuer rather than exposing his vulnerability. As a result, their mistrust for each other grew stronger and eventually killed the initial attraction. In our work, we call this "shame goes shopping."

My (Krish) mother was strong and over-possessive. Amana also has a strong and assertive personality. In the early years of our relationship, before we worked together, we often would spend time in Denmark, where Amana is from. She was working there at the time and I would come to stay with her between workshops. I did not feel at home there at all. I could not speak the language and I felt abandoned because she was so at home. Once, when we stopped at a gas station to fill our car, on her way to go in to pay, she explained to me how to pump the gas. I was already feeling out of sorts because in Denmark, I regress (it's much better now) because I don't speak Danish. At that moment, I was fully convinced that she was trying to control me just as all women always did. I reacted with anger and even said something about hating controlling women.

But then I had to laugh because in that instant, the whole pattern became very clear to me. First, I could see that I was simply reacting to my mother. Furthermore, I could see that her "controlling" side was just a response to my regressed helplessness.

She had an alcoholic father who behaved like an irresponsible child. Her response was to become very strong and efficient. Whenever I slipped into behaving in a way that reminded her of her father, her reaction would be to step in and take control. Those moments have been good reminders for me to look inside at what is happening instead of getting blindly lost in the reaction.

From my side (Amana), it is a continual learning to watch whenever my mistrust of men and their ability to deal with practical things of life gets provoked and I slip into taking over and simply doing what needs to be done. I am slowly learning to delegate many of the details I used to take care of and to let go when Krish does things in a different way than I would have done them. I actually enjoy the fact that we are so different and it is becoming easier to let go of having to control everything. In this example, our healing movement is for Krish to become more involved with the practical details of life and not just space out as was his survival strategy with his controlling mother. My healing movement is for me to be with the panic of my child when things are not getting done or are chaotic, instead of acting out into controlling and doing.

> *There is probably no other area where we regress so readily and become so emotional, disturbed, frantic, frustrated, desperate, and lost as when we are relating to our love partner. If we are simply willing to learn to recognize and get some distance from these feelings, trust will grow between us and our lover.*

It is one thing to know about our hurty and our childhood traumas and it is quite another to observe how this manifests itself today in our intimate relationships. When we can observe this dynamic in action, and choose to behave differently, we have made a significant step in our transformation.

Key #2 – Choosing Between Depth and Diversity

Recently, we did a session with a woman who felt that she could not trust her boyfriend because he occasionally slept with other women. She felt betrayed because they had made a verbal agreement not to be with others and he had broken it. Now, she was trying to decide how to deal with this betrayal and whether she wanted to continue seeing him. We began by exploring what it felt like for her when he did this and she began to touch her deep wound of shame and unworthiness as a woman. She admitted that she did not feel worthy of being with him because she felt that his energy was "higher" than hers and that he was a more attractive person than her.

She did not see that she might be a gift to him but could only see that his being with her was a gift to her. When we asked her to set the shamed part of her to the side and look at him more objectively, she realized clearly that he was not the kind of person who wanted to be with just one woman—at least not at that time. Then we asked her that if she accepted him as he was, including his desire to make love to other women, would she still want to be with him? She did. Her boyfriend was being who he was. But this decision did not last. A year later, she left because she valued herself enough to trust that what she needed was to be with someone who also had the desire to be with only one person sexually.

> *Whenever we become clear, it is important for us to make the choice between depth and diversity based on an honest assessment of our energy in the moment and be willing to face the consequences of our decision.*

However, it is not always easy to get clear whether we want to be in an exclusive one to one relationship or if we want variety. There are often two sides of us that want different things. One side does not want to disturb what we have. The other does not want to become stuck and mundane. When lovers get into conflict and don't know how to work with the energy that gets provoked, then resentments build up and they may stop communicating on a deeper level. Out of this place of hurt and anger that has not been expressed the energy may begin to wander toward other people.

It may suddenly seem very attractive to be with other men or women. When we get stuck in roles and the relating becomes dry, our energy wanders. When two people are not growing together, taking the relationship deeper, and building greater trust, it frequently happens that one or both will have an affair. Couples may find it easier to bind each other to a "commitment" rather than risk the possibility that one of them could have an affair. But that kind of an arrangement does not work, as it is based on an idea rather than on understanding.

A few years ago, two close friends of ours, who had been together as a couple for more than ten years, ran into trouble. He was attracted to another woman and once when she went away to another country for several months for work, he had an affair with this woman. It was a big shock because neither had had affairs before during their years together. But their relationship had become stale in fixed roles. He had become the provider and became withholding emotionally, while she became demanding, dependent, and clinging. Within this relating dynamic, both felt resentment and hurt for not being seen and understood, and they both felt betrayed. His affair with this new woman lasted off and on for over a year and neither of them knew if they wanted to continue or break up. Finally, his partner went away again on another work assignment and this time, she had an affair. Now, it was his turn to feel the pain of abandonment.

The emotional turmoil caused them both to investigate their own behaviors and explore what they needed to learn from the situation. They were forced to question the relationship they shared and see if they wanted to continue being together. It was a fruitful time for both of them. She came to understand that she had been giving up herself by becoming so dependent and it was important for her to find her own strengths apart from him. He could see that his provider role and his emotional withholding were old escape mechanisms and it was much more creative for him not to play the role of the caretaker but instead expose his own vulnerability. Now they are back together in a much stronger and healthier way, truly able to enjoy and appreciate each other.

In our own relationship, we have not felt any interest in sleeping with others. But it was not something that we decided; it was just something that we both felt. We had realized by the time we met that to enter into deep intimacy with a partner takes tremendous trust and that deep trust not only takes time to develop but also is very delicate and fragile. We have always felt so nourished by each other that we didn't feel the desire to go elsewhere.

> *Rules and verbal commitment are not what builds trust. It is truthfulness to ourselves and honesty toward the other person. We need to become honest with what we need and allow change if we notice that our needs are changing.*

We are all so different and we need different things at different times. Perhaps we find that deepening love and trust in a one to one relationship is more nourishing than being with many lovers. Perhaps we find just the opposite to be more nourishing. Or, as in the example above, a couple may have to go through a process like they did to get closer and clearer.

Key #3 – Trust Grows By Not Compromising Our Life Energy

A couple in a recent group had a habit of doing everything together. Wherever one went, the other went as well. They could hardly allow the other to have a different opinion. The woman complained that her husband prevented her from doing what she wanted to do. She claimed he was possessive and hindered her. She also criticized him for being so conventional and holding down her life energy. And to top it off, when he was playing games on the computer, she said that she felt disturbed and could not meditate because he did not inspire her spirituality.

This is called adult symbiosis. It is understandable and common among long-term partners but it can become suffocating and unhealthy. Both people have a difficult time allowing the other to separate and to have his or her life because it is so threatening. When we are scared to separate and take the space we need to be with ourselves, we may blame the other for not allowing us to separate. On an even deeper level, we may even discover that we have lost awareness of our own needs, feelings, and energy in our closeness with the other person. When we give up ourselves, we build resentment and stop trusting.

To build trust, we need to begin to discover what our life energy is saying even if it is not what the other person wants. This understanding is vital to being able to trust each other because when we stay true to our energy, we become trustworthy. If we find the courage to pursue our creativity, our friendships and our interests even if they are different from the other person's or even if they create conflict, then what we give to each other becomes more authentic. Compromising about important matters creates resentment and distance. Often, we give in or deny ourselves important things just to avoid conflict because we sense the other person's hidden demands or disapproval. These situations are trust breakers. We don't trust ourselves and the person cannot trust us either because he or she can never really be sure whether we are doing what we truly want to do or simply pleasing him or her out of fear of following our energy.

An example of a compromise could be that we stop seeing a friend that our partner does not like. Or we take more and more time away from some activity we enjoy doing because it takes us away from the other. Or we change our point of view to adjust to the other. Or we make love in a way that doesn't feel good because the other likes it. Or we make love when our body doesn't want to. Or we say things that we don't mean or feel. These concessions can be subtle but they erode the trust we have for ourselves and for the other because we are not being attentive to our own needs.

> *We have to risk honoring our own needs. This does not mean that in order to live or be close to another person we don't have to accommodate. But when we accommodate about essential things, it is no longer accommodation, it is compromise.*

Key # 4 – Developing Trust by Opening Our Vulnerability

There are three aspects to this key. One is a willingness to confront our fears of closeness and take risks to challenge those fears. The second is a willingness to share our story of shame and trauma and to listen and get to know that of our lover. And the third is a sincere willingness to become aware of our power games—our strategies of defense and vindictiveness.

a) Being Willing to Confront Our Fears of Opening

Just as we need to honor our needs and our energy, we also have to make a continual effort to penetrate our defenses. In the early period of a relationship, it is easier for two people to stay open to each other because there is still novelty and the mistrust wound has not yet been triggered. But over time, old patterns and protections grow. The closer the relationship, the greater are the fears of opening because we encounter deeper layers of shame and entitlement. As our childish expectations get disappointed, our resentment or resignation grows. For love to stay alive and growing, we have to make some efforts to keep opening more and more to the other person. When resentments build up or our fears of opening are provoked we may let life pull us into endless details and stresses and we can easily let days, weeks or months go by, obsessed and preoccupied and forget to connect with each other in a deep and meaningful way.

I (Krish) noticed for the first time in my relationship with Amana that after a certain amount of time "doing my own thing," I began to get an uneasy feeling inside. In the past, I would feel uneasy but it was mostly guilt. This time, I noticed that I was missing something. When I allowed time to go by without our coming close and connecting with each other, something began to feel strange and uncomfortable. For an anti-dependent person like me who has always been much more comfortable in his own world than in the world of relating, it has taken some adjustment to feel as nourished in togetherness as in "aloneness." I put the word "aloneness" in quotation marks because as an anti-dependent, I never really understood what aloneness meant. It was more a reaction to being engulfed and an avoidance of allowing someone to come close to me. Sharing does not necessarily mean talking. It is often more energetic than verbal and that seems to give me the space to both be with myself and with Amana. But I have to remind myself when I am losing myself in old ways of being such as unconsciously retreating into my world of compulsive doing, getting lost in my projects and forgetting to connect.

b) Getting to Know Each Other's Wounds

A big part of opening to each other also involves learning the other person's experience with abandonment and engulfment. We all have a part of us inside which longs to melt with someone and another part that needs to separate and be alone. When we deny one of those parts, we have a tendency to polarize and find the denied side in the other person. Once we recognize that we have both needs, it isn't enough just to be attentive to ourselves. We also learn to become sensitive to the needs of the other person. When differences arise, they can be resolved more easily when both people appreciate the need for closeness and nourishment and the need to spend time alone.

Because we have been wounded, it is a challenge to coordinate our different needs with those of another person in a love relationship—especially in terms of closeness and aloneness. In these areas, we are extremely sensitive to being rejected and disrespected. We each have our own version of being abandoned (of being deprived of essential needs at an early age) and being engulfed (not being supported to separate and individuate). When we know how each of our needs for love and nourishment may not have been met, we can more easily understand why we can be so sensitive and reactive today when we feel deprived of love and closeness. The same is true for feeling possessed or disrespected. Knowing our own wounds and those of the other helps us to avoid many misunderstanding and conflicts. However, we need to be careful not to simply understand this with our minds. What builds trust is knowing the other person's story and holding the wounded part of the other in our heart, as if we are taking in the person's pain and understanding him or her on a very deep level.

> *Trust grows when we know intimately our own story of trauma and that of the other person.*

We come to know the ways that we were distracted from ourselves, forced to abandon our real self and put on masks for love and approval—the ways that we were not valued, perhaps not even wanted, the ways we were humiliated, pressured, abused, programmed and repressed in our vital life energies. All of these experiences make up our story. And they determine the patterns that we live out in our current relating. From our story, we can identify the ways that our hurt gets triggered and comes up over and over again. We also recognize the same for our beloved.

I (Krish) have always been suspicious that the woman I am with is going to become overly possessive and sabotage my outside friendships. Not long into our relationship, we had a conflict about a woman who was a close friend of mine. Amana felt that this person was not respectful of our relationship but I felt that Amana was trying to pull me away from a close friend. I was so blinded by my experiences that I could not see anything clearly. This was a case where our wounds clashed. (What we call "Godzilla meets Frankenstein.") Amana felt patronized and disrespected by my woman friend, I felt controlled.

Fortunately, we both had enough space to allow this conflict to be there and see what it meant for each of us. For Amana, she needed to trust her feelings and to allow herself to be in her reaction, which meant not wanting to see or have anything to do with this woman for a while. For me, I needed to stand up for the fact that Amana was my woman and validate to her and to my friend that she felt disrespected. I also needed to allow myself to validate how important this friendship with my old friend was for me and to continue to see her and run the risk that Amana might disapprove. We could also share with each other what it brought up and how it triggered an old wound and listen to what the other person needed. In time, the wound healed and now the three of us have a close friendship and it's easy being together.

c) Becoming Aware of Our Power Games

The flip side of vulnerability is protection and power games. Habitually, in relationship, we move into games of protection and control whenever we feel disappointed, betrayed, or invaded. It takes a strong willingness to become aware of our power games and make a choice to drop them. We developed our power strategies as a way of trying to feel secure, safe, and strong in the world and with people. They give us a false sense of confidence and strength. And power games in our intimate relating build mistrust more strongly than any other dynamic between lovers. When we control, place demands upon, patronize, abuse, manipulate, guilt, deceive, lie to, disrespect or belittle another person, his or her trust for us disintegrates.

> *If we want trust, it is important to look at*
> *what we may be doing that makes it unsafe for*
> *the other person to open and be vulnerable.*

Recently, a woman came for a session disturbed because she was living in a house with three other women and felt that they were treating her disrespectfully. She wanted to know how to deal with this situation. We needed to explore many aspects to bring understanding to the situation. One was that it was a replica of an earlier relationship with her younger sister and her mother where her sister got most of her mother's energy and attention and she felt excluded. Another was that she was frightened around women who were strong, assertive, and not always respectful and it put her in a state of shock. She was able to explore these two dynamics easily. But she was not able to see the ways that she was also being disrespectful and aggressive with the other women. It was easy for her to see how they invaded her but very difficult for her to see how she invaded them. In fact, they were reacting to her demands, judgments, and expectations. She was angry and entitled but she couldn't see it.

Sometimes, our power maneuvers can be so engrained, habitual, automatic, and unconscious that we are not in touch with them at all. All too often, we focus on what the other person does that makes us close down. But remaining focused on the other person's power games is an escape from looking at ourselves and from seeing how our behavior may be partly responsible for how the other person is behaving. If we wait for the other person to drop their power games and open first, we may be waiting a very long time. As soon as we are willing to look at our own behavior honestly and openly, the energy changes. Usually the moment the other person feels this willingness, opening happens. Otherwise, the other person feels more and more hurt and wounded and pulls away. They may not know why or even that they are pulling away but they no longer feel safe.

A man in a group was sharing that he was still angry and hurt because a year previously, his wife had left him. He was angry because she had an affair with another man while they were still together without telling him and then finally left him without an explanation. When we began to explore the situation more deeply, he revealed that his mother had been very abusive toward him as a child but now in his relationships, he was playing the role of the abuser. He could not see how his control and aggression was intimidating his wife or why, because of this energy, she stopped opening to him, was too afraid to be honest, and finally left him. All he felt was that he was being rejected for being vulnerable and open.

> *Our power games are fueled by our fears of*
> *abandonment and by our fears of invasion.*

Looking at our shadow sides—our aggression, irritability, hidden resentments, controlling or tyrannical behaviors, seductiveness, dishonesty, competitiveness and vengefulness is much more difficult that exploring our wounds. Usually they are cloaked in self-judgment and denial. It is not easy to accept these qualities and forgive ourselves for having them. But they are just covers for our fears and wounds. The deeper we go in understanding the ways that we were traumatized and shamed, the easier it becomes to see them in a loving light and to understand that they were and are our survival strategies. We may not need them anymore but we certainly needed them earlier in life.

Key #5 Taking Responsibility for Our Own Fulfillment

Most of us have been so deeply conditioned by the romantic dream, that we have come to believe that magical fulfillment awaits us when we find "the one." When we import that fallacy into our relationships, it is an almost certain blueprint for disaster.

On the contrary, if we want our relating to deepen and flourish, we need to discover our own creative and spiritual fulfillment.

In our work, we often encounter lovers who have not taken these steps on their own and depend on the other person or the relationship to fill this hole inside. From our experience, each of us needs to continually look inside and to give to ourselves whatever we need to meet our creative and spiritual needs.

> *To truly be able to cherish the other person and recognize his or her unique gifts, we need to fill fulfilled in our own life or at least be taking positive steps toward our personal fulfillment.*

We need to express our creativity or be with ourselves in a way that brings us joy separate from the other person. If we put everything on the relating and expect the other person to bring us that fulfillment, we destroy the delicate flower of love.

Key #6 – Opening to Aloneness

This brings us to the final key that in some ways is the most difficult key of all because it forces us to confront our profound fears of abandonment, rejection, and isolation. We have already discussed this topic in a previous chapter but it is so essential to the possibility of trust between lovers that it is important to mention again in this context. When we are willing to face our aloneness, we create a foundation for love and trust to flourish because the other person does not feel that he or she has to give up their freedom in order to receive our love. When we have a **willingness** to face the frustration of the other's not being as we want the person to be, the other person begins to feel that our love is no longer conditional. This is the greatest gift we can give to ourselves and to the one we love.

Exercise:

Ask yourself:

1. *How does my regressed child act out in my intimate relationship(s)?*

2. *At this time in my life, do I choose to be sexually exclusive with one person or do I want something else? If so, am I willing to clear and honest about my choice?*

3. *If I am close to someone, am I willing to honor my own needs and not sacrifice them for the sake of the relationship?*

4. *Am I willing to make a constant effort to open my vulnerability with the person I am close to?*

5. *Am I willing to look honestly at my power games and choose to find another way to be and communicate?*

6. *Am I willing to contain my frustration when I am not getting what I want?*

7. *Am I relying on the relationship to fulfill me?*

* * *

CHAPTER 13:

RITUALS OF REPAIR –

Repairing Disharmony in Our Relating

That's exactly what love is:
Two persons are trying to solve life's problems together.
Each relationship is a growth opportunity.
Don't condemn it, enjoy it in all its phases –
in the moments when everything is beautiful and
in the moments when everything is dark.
That's how life is, ups and downs.
Osho

In any significant relationship, there are going to be times of disconnection and conflict. Any two people will not always agree on important aspects of their life together. Sometimes one person's needs and desires conflict directly with the other person's. Sometimes we may feel that we are right, (and we may be) but our partner does not see it that way. And he or she may be just as convinced of being right. How to deal with these inevitable moments?

I remember a joke my uncle, the raconteur of the family, once told.

Two women meet on the street. They haven't seen each other for some time.

One says to the other, "So…how is your marriage?

"Not so good. We got divorced a couple of years ago. What about yours?"

"Great. We have been married for twenty-five years and still going strong."

"How on earth are you managing?"

"Well, when we got married, we made an agreement. He would decide about the big things and I would decide about the smaller things in life. He would decide about immigration and reform, whether we should negotiate with China, when we should recognize Cuba, and if we should have universal health care. I would decide where we should live, what house we should buy, what car to buy, and how many children to have. This agreement worked out great."

Most couples don't have it so good. But all is not lost.

> *What distinguishes a healthy relationship from a dysfunctional one is not whether there are conflicts and disagreements but whether there is a willingness to take responsibility for what we contribute to any conflict and a deep commitment to repair disharmony.*

When conflict and hurt arise, we may have an instinctual habit of closing down and reinforcing our mistrust beliefs. When that happens, our mistrust deepens as well as our conviction that it is useless to open and the belief that we will always end up being hurt even more. But, if we see relationship as a growth experience and know from the start that we are going to get triggered in our most sensitive places, our focus changes. If we enter every significant relationship in our life knowing that we are bringing our mistrust and that it will be provoked at some point, everything changes. Then, rather than expecting perpetual harmony, we anticipate that conflicts will arise and even welcome them as a chance to grow.

The child in us wants and expects to get what he or she wants and expects. He or she even feels absolutely justified in receiving it. When we are disappointed, we will react in predictably childish ways. We rant and rave, shut down, get cold, get hot, get moody, analyze, blame, accuse, or attack, all the time feeling "right." "If he/she loves me, don't you think he/she should do this or that?' is a common refrain we hear from couples who are in conflict. The most dangerous result of this kind of attitude and behavior is that it can go on for years. And during that time, the suffering, resentment, and bitterness grow. Relationships take work, constant work.

If we don't commit to this, they will go downhill. It is a bit like keeping a house clean. If we don't make the continual effort to keep it fresh and clean, it gets dirty and pretty soon it starts to stink. A relationship is no different. We worked with a couple in Germany who had been together for twelve years and were in both cold and hot war with each other. When they came to see us, both were unsure they wanted to stay together even though they had two children. He felt that after the birth of their children, she cut off emotionally from him and ceased to be available to connect or to make love as they used to. He questioned if she still loved him because he no longer felt "special," "attractive," or "desired" by her. And he no longer felt she valued him as a man.

From her side, she was fed up with his demands and expectations. She felt chronically criticized, judged, and blamed by him. She said that he came to her not in a loving way, but to get something and was never satisfied. She claimed that he had no idea what it took to care for two children. And now, rather than have two children to take care of, she felt she had three. As we continued to work with them, their complaints of each other only became more numerous and more heated. The trust between them had broken down. They were both totally on the defensive, shut down, and angry.

In our experience, there are two aspects of repair, both of which are vital. The first is what we call "the inner process" and the second, we call "the repairing process." In the first stage, we go in and explore what in our own wounds and past have been triggered. Our focus in the inner process is to take responsibility for how we may have contributed to the conflict and mistrust and see what lesson we need to learn. In the second, we approach the other person with a willingness and a commitment to repair. In the repair process, we come not as an angry child but in what we call, "the adult state of consciousness"—open, vulnerable, willing to share our own hurt without blame, and willing to listen to the other person's hurt.

We refer to this whole process, both the first and the second, as "rituals of repair" for two reasons. First, we call it a ritual because there is something sacred about being willing to return to love and not stay in fight. Second, we call it a ritual because it needs to become a habit, almost like second nature, not to allow discord and dissention to grow and fester but to deal with it immediately. The inner process may take a little while but just the willingness and the understanding to not minimize conflicts but to look at the situation and feel what it triggers in us changes something.

The Adult and the Child States of Consciousness

Before we can go further, we need to understand more precisely the difference between what we call, "the child state of consciousness" and "the adult state of consciousness." When we are disturbed, frustrated, disappointed, and hurt, we enter v automatically into the child state of consciousness. In this state, our deep mistrust is triggered, together with underlying shame, loneliness, and fear. But rather than stop and feel the fear, shame or loneliness, we usually get angry and move into an expectation and a reaction.

Most often, we don't make the connection between the frustration and disturbance we are feeling and the fear, shame or loneliness underneath. We remain focused on feeling wronged by the other person, feeling misunderstood, on feeling that he or she *"should"* not be this way and something needs to change. Then naturally, when we go to the other person, he or she receives this energy and feels blamed. That is the child state of consciousness. In this consciousness, as we mentioned in the chapter on the regressed child, we think and behave just as a child would. If we were to reflect even for a moment, feel our energy, and observe our behavior, we would notice without any doubt that we are being taken over by our child inside.

The adult state of consciousness is very different. We may still be emotional and disturbed, but we have taken time to cool down and reflect. In the child state, we are highly emotional and reactive; in the adult state, we are reflective and responsive. The child is impatient and impulsive; the adult is patient and considers the whole situation. The adult consciousness has the ability to contain frustration and to not act automatically from our impulses. It can see the whole situation that provoked us, not simply in terms of our own hurt and unmet needs, but also considering the other person's feelings and needs. In the adult state, we can validate our needs but recognize that if we come to the other person in anger and expectation, we will not have those needs met. The adult in us also knows that an angry, expecting child cannot communicate; it can only vent frustration. Finally, the adult is willing to listen, to take in the other person, to respect him or her as a unique being who deserves to be listened to because his or her feelings are important.

> *The act of listening is a choice we can make.*
> *It is a gift we give to another person and, in*
> *itself, it solves many problems.*

Processing Our Betrayals

When we begin a process of self-discovery, we may not even be aware of how much we have gone into resignation with the people close to us in our life. It takes a lot of honest looking at ourselves to be able to see this clearly. But when we pay close attention, we can observe how our life energy goes down when we don't express when we are hurt or disappointed. We can observe how we may have pulled back from the person we feel hurt by, maybe even to the point of cutting them off. We can observe how we may be judging that person or invalidating the friendship or love we have for him or her. If it is a lover, we can observe how our sexual energy may have diminished or disappeared. We can feel how our trust has been damaged. In all these ways, we bring light to the hurt we hold in our heart.

> *To live passionately and to return to a natural flow of our life energy means we need to reverse the dysfunctional relating habits we learned as a child.*

When we start to validate our feelings and our self-worth, we begin to realize that our hurt is important enough to feel and to express. Life is short and time is precious. If we allow our hurts to go unprocessed and if we don't care enough about ourselves and our relationships, we may find ourselves one day feeling extremely isolated and alone and regretting that we didn't say things when we had a chance to.

We call this approach, "making it matter." When we "make it matter," it usually means feeling hurt. One of the reasons that we close off and don't express our hurt is because we don't want to feel the hurt or we are afraid of the consequences if we express it. Sometimes our pride interferes with allowing us to feel the hurt. It may be easier to pretend that the person doesn't count to us than it is to admit that we care enough to feel hurt. We close down to the other person because we don't want to feel the ways that we hurt him or her or the way that they have hurt us. It could mean seeing a part of ourselves that is difficult to look at.

When we allow ourselves to feel the hurt and the way our heart may have closed down, the next step is to expose our hurt. Often when we first begin expressing hurt, it comes out as blame. When our wounded child expresses hurt, it is usually looking for someone to make responsible for the pain. But if we are willing to go beyond blame and feel our hurt, our pain, our shame or our fears, realizing that our hurt is much older than the current situation, it can be very creative even to start with expressing our blame, anger and frustration. Then the anger and hurt becomes a doorway to deepen our love.

It is not always practical or appropriate to share your hurt with the person who has provoked your betrayal. The person may have died, or is unavailable or unwilling to receive it or we may be too frightened and intimidated to approach him or her. But we can still allow ourselves to come out of resignation, to feel our passion and hurt in the absence of the person, in a safe and neutral environment perhaps with a friend or therapist. The important thing is that we are feeling and expressing this energy for ourselves.

We are not doing this to change the other person in any way. The other person is simply a mirror that has shown us something inside of us that needs to be brought to the light so it can heal.

After we have felt and expressed the anger, we begin to feel the hurt. Then we are no longer focused on the other. We are no longer a victim. It is our pain and it has been there a long time. The other person is merely the trigger of this hurt. We become aware that this betrayal experience reminds us of an earlier time when we felt betrayed in a similar way. When we connect deeply with the original betrayal, it releases tremendous energy that then becomes available to us in the present. It is not that we need to keep going back to re-experience the trauma and pain but simply that whatever triggers us in our life today is an opportunity to release the energy still locked in the past.

Making this connection allows us to take responsibility for our life and to recognize that in a bigger and wiser perspective, we are living and watching an unfolding of a story. This story has a beginning with our original traumas. It has a middle with the re-enactment of our traumas. And it has an end when we allow ourselves to deeply feel the pain and the fear, when we accept our woundedness, and when we embrace our trauma with love and compassion, understanding, and acceptance of our humanness. This is the story of coming back home to ourselves again; of learning the lessons we need to learn.

The Inner Process

(For several years, we have been studying and training in the work of Marshall B. Rosenberg, PhD, called *Nonviolent Communication*. In developing both the "Inner Process" and "Repair Process" which follow, we have been deeply influenced by his techniques and we have adapted it to our work.)

Here are some steps to guide you in the process of going in. It is not a linear formula but it helps to have some tools.

1. Begin by looking at *what specific action or inaction* on the part of the other person provoked your anger, disappointment, hurt, or frustration.

Feel the anger and the hurt in your body. Feel the compulsion to do something, to attack the person or to tell him or her that they are wrong and should change. If necessary, (and it usually is necessary) separate from the other person, take a walk, or spend time alone in whatever way is appropriate and possible.

2. Ask yourself, "What is the *expectation* that I have which is not being met right now?"

Expectations repel, vulnerability attracts.

3. Ask yourself, "What is the *fear* if I don't get this expectation met?"

If we observe ourselves carefully, we may be able to detect fear. Anger is a cover for fear. But anger feels differently than fear. Anger makes us feel hot in the body, tightens the belly, and causes us to move fast, raise our voice, or act impulsively and impetuously. Fear is a step deeper. It can cause contraction in the chest or belly, tightness in the solar plexus, racing repetitive and compulsive thoughts, mental confusion, or spacing out.

4. Ask yourself, "What is *the basic need* that I fear will not be met, which this situation is provoking?" (This is a tricky step because when we begin to focus on our unmet needs, we can easily fall into the belief that it is the other person's responsibility to meet it. But the point is to allow yourself to connect deeply and to validate this basic need.)

> *Getting in touch with the unmet need(s) that are arising in the situation that disturbs us is in order to understand ourselves more deeply; and to develop deeper compassion for ourselves. It is not to justify how the other person should change.*

Here is a list of possible basic needs that may have been triggered:

a) *The need for safety, protection, and security*
b) *The need for love and connection*
c) *The need to feel autonomy and to feel supported in that autonomy*
d) *The need to feel validated in your feelings*
e) *The need to feel touched with presence and sensitivity*
f) *The need to have your "no" respected*
g) *The need to feel listened to, taken in and heard*
h) *The need for honesty*
i) *The need for commitment*
j) *The need for relaxation and playtime*

5. Allow yourself to *feel the pain of all the times in your past* that this need was not met. Be as specific as you can with past memories when this situation and these feelings came up before so that you can feel the pain of what you went through and recognize that pattern that you are creating in your current relationships.

Most of the time, we don't do any of the above. Instead, we react. The man in the couple above would get angry and yell, slam doors, storm out of the house, and then come back and complain. The woman would just shut down, refuse to talk, and keep herself busy with other things. Slowly, she began to spend more and more time with her friends and not even tell him where and what she was doing.

In the session, after they both had expressed their discontent and grievances, we focused on how these situations for each of them was provoking a deep wound inside. He was seeing how he was expecting her to fill his insecurity as a man and rather than feel it, he was blaming her. He needed to learn to contain his frustration when he was not getting what he expected in terms of nourishment and attention. If he truly owned his own shame and neediness, he might approach her in vulnerability rather than with anger and expectation. If he came to her from a space of wanting rather than giving, he would invariably receive rejection.

In her case, she needed to learn to set appropriate limits. She lost herself in relationship with a man, gave up her own life, and assumed the role of a caretaker. When he blamed and criticized her and projected his expectation on her, if she did not clearly stand up for her truth, she would naturally build resentment. In the place of a clear limit, she became passive aggressive and cut him off.

The Repair Process

We asked him to ask her, using his own words,

"How can I communicate my feelings and what is going on inside of me, without your feeling that I am making a demand or putting pressure on you?"

"That's exactly the problem. I feel that you want me to change," she answered.

"OK, I see that. But I can't live without getting love and respect from you."

"I cannot respond to your pressure. First of all, when you come with this energy that I have to change, I close off."

"I just want to have a dialogue with you," he said.

"It's not a dialogue. You tell me what's wrong with me, you tell me what I should do differently, and you analyze me. You go on and on. That's why I don't want to have talks with you."

She felt relieved that she was able to clearly say what was closing her down. This was an important lesson for her, part of her moving into her adult state.

At this point, we helped him to see that he could not get the love he wanted in the way he was behaving and talking to her. He could understand. Slowly, he was moving into his adult state.

We ended the session with both of them seeing how they had behaved as a child with each other and making a commitment to learn a new way and would work with deepening their repair tools in subsequent sessions.

When we have connected to the wound that has been triggered, and take responsibility for the hurt, realizing that our partner is only the trigger and not the source, we are ready for repair. It is also important to feel that returning to the love between you and your partner is the goal and all else is secondary. We can come to repair when we have connected with the adult space that has decided that love is a priority. We usually teach: "You can be right or you can have love. You can't have both at the same time."

Here are the steps we suggest:

1. You can begin the repair process when you have reached a place inside where you are no longer *charged* and ready to approach the other person with *a clear intention to create love and connection.* Start by making a commitment to yourself *to share without blame,*

attack, analysis, accusation, or wanting to fix or change the other person.

(If you still want to do any of the above, go back to the inner process. If necessary, talk to a trusted friend first if you cannot get out of the child state of consciousness.)

2. Begin by saying to your partner, *"I would like to share something. Do you have the space to listen?"*

If the other person does not have the space at this time, you can ask the person to let you know when he or she has the space to listen.

3. When the other person has the space to listen, then say, the following in your own words:

"I am feeling hurt/disconnected/upset and I would like to try to reconnect with you and repair."

"When you did or didn't, said or didn't say, I felt."

Keep it short and precise.

Refer to a very specific action or statement that happened and remain factual without interpretation or analysis. Also, avoid saying, "You made me feel, or it made me feel." Simply say, "I felt." When you describe your feeling, try to keep it simple such as, "I felt hurt or sad or disappointed." At this point, you can also talk about how this situation triggered memories and feelings from your past so that the other person can understand that this is your process. Again, try to keep it simple and to the point.

4. The next step is to connect the feeling to a basic need. You can say,

"When this happened, or when you said or did that, it triggers a basic need inside of me that I am afraid will not be met and it opens a wound for me from all the times in my past when this basic need was not met."

Say what the basic need is.

In talking about the need that was not met, also talk about how this need was not met in the past and about your insecurity that you deserve to have it met and fears that it will never be met.

5. The next step, if it is appropriate, is to make a request of the person. This request could be to ask the person, *"I wonder if you would be willing to tell me what you heard me say and if you would be willing to tell me how you feel when I say this?"*

In making this request, make sure that it is not a demand. And you can know the difference if you are willing to receive a no. Also, make the request specific so the other person is clear what you would like.

6. Now, invite the other person to share, following the same steps.

When we are guiding this structure, we also spend some time teaching the person who is receiving, how to listen. It is good to remember that in the child consciousness, we cannot listen. Instead, we are impatient to get our point of view across, and want to defend ourselves, especially if we feel guilty or wronged. The child wants to be right! Sometimes, it is simply a matter of choosing to shift to the adult state of consciousness. Other times we need to spend time with ourselves; to soothe ourselves before we may be able to listen. In the adult state, we open our heart to receive the other person's sharing and feel his or her feelings and needs as he or she shares.

Repairing When We Have Done Harm

The situation of repair is slightly different when we have actually done or said something that was harmful to the other person such as losing our temper, or being invasive or disrespectful. In this case, we have to make amends. We have to repair the trust that we damaged by what we have said or done. An apology is not enough. We have to feel the pain we have caused and the other person has to feel that we can feel that pain; furthermore, we have to make a sincere commitment to ourselves and to the other to deal with whatever it is inside that causes us to act in this way. And the other person has to feel that commitment.

For instance, the wife of a couple who came for a workshop shared that her husband said to her that he was disgusted by the weight she was gaining. She said that he told her that he was no longer attracted to her because her belly was starting to stick out. We turned to the husband and asked him if it was true that he had said these things. He admitted that he had and that he felt ashamed for saying it and for exposing it to the group.

"Are you sensing that this might have an effect on the trust between you?" we asked.

"Yes, of course I do, but sometimes I just can't control myself."

We worked with his own deep shame that was underneath and the way his self-image was dependent on how his woman looked to him and to others. We suggested that he continue to work on this issue in individual therapy. Then we asked him if he felt to apologize to her in front of the group. At first, his apology was not deep or sincere enough to touch her but, with time, he could reach the place inside where he could feel the pain he had caused and his own shame that made it so important for him how his woman looked.

"Are you willing to commit to her that you won't repeat this kind of behavior?" we asked.

"Yes, I will try."

"Trying is not really good enough," we said. "You have to mean it if you want her trust to heal and your love to continue."

"I promise to you," he told her, "that this will never ever happen again."

(This case was a success story for both of them. This incident happened two years ago. He was in weekly therapy for a year, working on his shame and his anger with women. His treatment of his wife changed dramatically as did their relationship.)

Reaching Out for Help

There is one final aspect to the repair process. If it is not possible to listen and to feel each other, if disharmony and disconnection is deepening because we are lost in our hurt, *then it is time to reach out for help*. We have worked with many couples that have not taken this step. In their trying to resolve conflict, they can't seem to find their way out of the child state of consciousness. All they do is blame, attack and accuse each other. In short, they lacked the tools to resolve conflicts and allowed their pain, mistrust, and resentments to grow. Then it can become too late to repair. Sometimes couples get so used to suffering in disharmony, creating greater and greater distance from each other that they forget that there is an alternative. With children, financial concerns and the fear of being alone, couples are often willing to put up with this painful disharmony.

There's only one reason that makes repair impossible. That is the unwillingness to do the inner work that it requires. It is not in our nature to live together with someone in unresolved disharmony, but we have to do what it takes to restore love. If we can't do it alone, then we need to seek professional help. Not all couples can stay together. Each person may have very different priorities in life. But when we decide to separate from the adult state of consciousness, it comes with a lot of gratitude for the time spent together, a deep love for the other person and for the richness they brought into our life. Separation from this space allows for a natural deep grieving process of letting go and creating space for something new for both partners.

Exercise:

Ask yourself:

1. *When conflict arises in my intimate relating, am I willing to go inside and do the inner process described in this chapter?*

2. *Am I willing to come to my partner after my inner process to repair the conflict?*

* * *

PART 4:

TRUST AND INTELLIGENCE

CHAPTER 14:

INNER AND OUTER GUIDES –

Our Journey from Mystification to Intelligence

*I have been making every effort
to make you aware of your individuality,
your freedom, your absolute capacity
to grow without any help from anyone.
Your growth is something intrinsic to your being.
It does not come from outside,
It is an unfolding.*
Osho

In any situation where we open, whether it is with a lover, a friend, a teacher, a therapist, or a guru, we go through the similar stages that we have been describing—initial caution (global mistrust), then exuberant and joyful opening and feelings of trust (fantasy trust), then betrayal and disappointment. If we work through these stages with understanding instead of getting stuck with blaming the other, we can reach a state of real trust.

Most often, in order to overcome our initial mistrust, when we find someone we feel we can trust, we idealize that person.

We become mystified. We place him or her on a pedestal and do not see clearly who this person is. This phenomenon of mystification is almost unavoidable because most of us have a deep longing to surrender. And, this process of mystification has a beautiful aspect to it. To grow emotionally and spiritually, most of us will need to reach out. To grow, we have to take the risk, drop our guard and defenses, and allow ourselves to be open. If we don't, it is hard, perhaps impossible, to get out of our old conditioning, to experience ourselves in new and refreshing ways, to open and work through our wounds and reach new states of consciousness and awareness. Without support, it is too easy for us to hide in our ego defenses and never open to new realities in our being.

Perhaps there is no arena where this process is more intense and more significant than in our spiritual growth. When we open to a spiritual teacher, a therapist, or a master, we bear our soul in its most vulnerable place.

> *The stakes are higher in the arena of spiritual and emotional growth than any other because we are opening places inside which are the deepest and most sacred of our being.*

Our search for truth, peace, and meaning in life is profound and impassioned. And because this area is so deep and significant, every part of us believes that the person we open to should absolutely not betray the trust we give to him or her. He or she should "walk the talk" with total integrity. A spiritual teacher should be authentic and respect our limits exquisitely. Furthermore, we also believe that it is the responsibility of the teacher not to create dependence in his students or disciples, but to empower them to discover their own intelligence. In a perfect world, this might be the case. But it is far from how it is in the world in which we live. Many teachers get trapped in their egos, abuse their power, and foster dependence rather than helping their students to work through the dependency to reach maturity and awaken the natural intelligence that we all have.

> *Ultimately, it is our own responsibility to recover our inner guide. An authentic teacher is one who guides us to discover this lost part of ourselves. If we open to a teacher, we may be betrayed or at least feel betrayed. But we can use this experience to help us to come home to our own truth.*

At some point, we have to take back our power and integrate the guidance we are receiving and make it our own. If we have felt betrayed, it is also our responsibility not to use this experience as an excuse to close down but to process our hurt and stay open. Ultimately, this is about our opening to existence, to life itself and through that to experience that life is holding us in its hands. This is the trust that we are all longing for and which we feel as a deep missing inside.

Krish's Story

I would like to share in some detail the process that I have been through in this arena because it has been a process that reflects the stages we have been discussing of recovering trust—initial mistrust, followed by mystification, then an experience of betrayal, and the final stage of discovering mature, real trust.

Thirty years ago, I was working as a family doctor and therapist in Laguna Beach, a small town in Southern California. I had been exploring different spiritual paths including yoga and Vipassana meditation and had been with different therapists but I had not yet opened deeply to a spiritual master. I had been very driven in my schooling but after graduating from college and medical training, I was deeply dissatisfied inside and knew that there was more to life than career, success, and family life. I had a driving search for truth that had taken me toward psychedelic drugs and human potential workshops but I knew there was even more to find. I was attracted to a specific spiritual teacher in India because of what I had heard about his radical ideas and methods. In fact, I was so attracted that I left my practice and life in California for a spiritual adventure without any clear plan of when I would return.

When I arrived at the ashram, I encountered a wild scene of many hundreds of people dressed in red robes following a spiritual master then named Bhagwan Shree Rajneesh and later "Osho." The people there seemed to be relating to each other in a very friendly, free, and loose way but I felt like a total outsider and nobody was going out of his or her way to make me feel welcomed. The program at the ashram included a morning discourse by Osho in which he commented on a text from different spiritual traditions or answered questions from disciples. There was also a large variety of therapy and meditation groups to choose from. The particular program you chose generally followed the recommendation of people working in the front office who evaluated you "intuitively."

I was highly skeptical and not a little frightened by the whole scene; yet still curious. So, I enrolled in a series of courses and began attending the morning discourses. In the lectures, Osho spoke frequently about what it meant to find oneself and to become free, silent, and meditative. In order to learn to go deeply into meditation, he was saying, it was necessary to begin by breaking away from our conditioning, which kept us imprisoned in old repressive beliefs, and learn to live our lives fully. He also said that harsh discipline only strengthened our egos and that it was much more important to let go and live. This touched me because I had spent years being very rigorous in my yoga and meditative practice and was feeling a bit dried out. He taught that we were not there to worship or follow him but only to find ourselves.

I began taking therapy groups that were much more radical than what I had been used to in California. In these groups, I was learning to explore my sexuality freely and to express feelings such as anger and pain_more openly than I had in the past. Over the next few weeks, I began to sense that I fit there and in some strong way, that I had come home. I decided to become initiated as a disciple. Initiation meant receiving a new name and a "mala" (a necklace of 108 wooded beads, one for each different method of meditation and locket with a picture of the master). When my name was called, I went up and looked into Osho's eyes. What I saw shocked me profoundly. I had the overwhelming feeling that there was no one there, that when I looked into his eyes, it was like looking into the universe. Yet this "nobody there" person was talking to me personally. He was saying that I didn't need to be looking so intensely for God. It was enough for me just to enjoy life and God would find me. Then he asked me how long I was planning to stay. First I said four months (which had been my plan) but no sooner had the words come out of my mouth before I added, "or maybe forever."

"Forever is a bit longer," I heard him say back to me.

Over the next few months, I became deeply involved in the life of the commune. I did more therapy and meditation groups and then was assigned to work as a carpenter (for which I had about as much skill as an elephant). I didn't particularly like the work but I definitely liked being a part of this commune. My devotion to Osho was growing although I was never a particularly devotional kind of person. I had the feeling that I was sitting in the presence of truth and this feeling was deeply nourishing, more nourishing than anything I had ever experienced before. I had such a deep longing to hear the truth but I had never heard it spoken before. Now I was not only hearing it spoken but I was also feeling it. In addition, the experience of being a disciple seemed more real to me than anything I had done before. In fact, my search for truth up to then seemed just like an idea by comparison. But it also wasn't easy. I was insecure, out of control and full of doubts and I hated being an inept carpenter. I longed to get back to doing something that I was good at and waited patiently to be invited to begin leading therapy groups.

About ten months after I had first arrived, the commune moved from India to America. Only a few hundred people were invited to come during the early stages of this new community but perhaps because I was a doctor and they needed doctors, I was asked. In America, we began to build a city in the Oregon wilderness—homes and office buildings, a therapy center, a huge meditation hall, a mall with shops and restaurants, two large cafeterias, a farm to grow our own food, a dairy, a medical center, and a hotel. It took four years and during that time, we worked as much as sixteen hours a day. We had little contact with Osho because he had gone into silence and seclusion. Once a day, though, he drove by to greet us on his way for a drive in the Oregon countryside.

One day, I had an opportunity to see him personally in connection with some work I was doing in the medical center. I had never been alone with him before; I was extremely nervous and I had no idea what to expect. As I went in, he greeted me and I found myself feeling at ease almost immediately. The room where he was sitting was beautiful but had no furniture except his chair and a stereo system. I find it difficult to describe the silence and stillness in that room. Our time together passed by very simply and when I left, he thanked me for coming. It felt to me as though nothing much had happened but I left feeling profoundly peaceful inside.

However, as the years went by, something strange and incomprehensible began to happen in the community. The leaders became more and more tyrannical. There was greater conflict with the American government and with the local and state authorities. Part of the controversy was stoked because our community and the things that Osho was teaching were highly controversial. But also, the woman who ran the commune was being provocative during the television interviews she was having. On the pretext that we needed to defend ourselves against a possible attack from government authorities, they formed a security force of people who carried semi-automatic weapons.

What had started out as an innocent and joyful experiment was turning into a nightmare. Eventually, things came to a head. One night, all the women who were running the commune left. I will probably never know the true story of what actually happened and I have long ago stopped being interested. But I did learn about some of the events. Apparently, the women had become overtaken by their paranoia and had been wire tapping all the phone lines to monitor communications to and from the commune, digging escape tunnels from their own living quarters, planning assassinations of government authorities, and other such atrocities. Osho said he was unaware of any of this and called in the FBI to investigate but the authorities also directed their energies toward him and finally deported him from the U.S. Shortly afterward, the commune in America ended.

I felt shattered inside. My dreams of living in a spiritual community with fellow seekers under the guidance of an enlightened person were shattered. I felt utterly betrayed because even if Osho didn't know most of what was happening, it was still his choice to pick the women who ran the place and it was, after all, his commune. I also felt angry and hurt because I had given my trust and I felt that he had betrayed it. I went back to California and took a job working as a doctor in an urgent care center. A few months later, I began a psychiatry residency at the same hospital where I had trained as a family doctor. Meanwhile, after traveling for a year in search of a new place to build a commune, Osho was forced to return to India to the site of the original commune because the American government prevented his being admitted to any other country. I had contact with old friends who went there but I was too wounded to even consider going back.

Two years passed, during which time, I maintained a distant contact. Slowly, I noticed that in spite of my hurt and my doubts, the pull to return was still there. My relationship with Osho was not over. Also, in my residency, I started to learn about early life wounds of abandonment and how we re-enact them in our life today. This gave me a different perspective of what had happened and I began to see that it had provoked buried wounds in me that needed healing. I could see that my feelings of betrayal with the master were a strong mirror of these primal wounds. In the beginning of my last third of the residency, I took a month off and went to India for a visit. When the month was over and I was leaving to return to the U.S., I knew I would be coming back soon. Two months after receiving my diploma, once again, just as I had done ten years before, I left a therapy practice, a home, and a relationship that was ending and went back to India.

I still had doubts. My heart was melting again but my mind wanted answers. At one point, I did a short workshop that a teacher/friend of mine designed for people who had been through the American experience and were coming back. On the last day, Osho's personal secretary came in and shared with us something that he had recently said to her. He told her that in the evening when he came out to talk to us, he could recognize people who had been in the commune in America. He was very touched to see our faces again. He knew what we had been through and how much we had suffered. He wanted us to know that we had been through one of the deepest tests that a master can give to his disciples. He told her that he had been using each of his communes as devices to teach us. In the first, we were learning how to live and transform our life energy and particularly our sexuality. In the second, he was teaching us about the nature of power and the political mind. And in the final commune, we were learning about meditation and death.

I don't know why but hearing these words opened something so deep in my heart that I cried for an hour. I have never cried like that before or since. After that moment, my mind stopped needing answers about the experience in America. I understood very deeply that everything I was experiencing with my master was a mirror of my inner process. There was nothing to mistrust or to react to on the outside because fundamentally, there was no outside. In those precious moments, I felt a profound experience of inner knowing and letting go. At the moment of surrender, I felt overtaken with love and gratitude and those moments have stayed with me since.

A few months after that experience, Osho left his body. I continued to live in the commune for a few more years. Without the master in his physical presence, I needed to let go of having a person to ask questions to and to see and listen to each day—to let go of the physical form of the master. But eventually, I discovered that there was a hidden blessing in his departure. It has encouraged me to slowly discover that the guidance I looked for on the outside is now inside.

This discovery has also opened me to the possibility of learning from teachers without the same quality of mystification. It has been a process of seeing that I can learn without giving up my power and my intelligence. I have on occasion gone to learn from different teachers. But I can see that something has changed profoundly for me. I cannot give away my power and my intelligence any longer. That time is over. I don't have to idealize or diminish the teachers whom I learn from. I can take what they have to teach and see them much more clearly for who they are both with their gifts and their shortcomings.

Amana's Story

I (Amana) would like to share an aspect of my process of learning to trust my spirituality and discover my inner guide. It involves an incident in which Krish and I reached a crisis because it appeared for a time that our spiritual paths were diverging. I have had several big challenges I passed through during our years together and each one has strengthened my trust in myself although at times during these challenges it has felt like I was passing through hell and wouldn't survive another day.

In 1998, when I had been with Krish for five years and we had just bought a house together in Sedona, I started moving away from the spiritual community that we were both a part of. We had originally come to Sedona to be part of this community. A woman we had met and worked with in India inspired it. Shortly after we bought our house, she was diagnosed with cancer and she died within a year. Her work was inspired by our spiritual master, Osho, and she was working with methods to apply his teachings to everyday living. She had created a mystery school that had a certain hierarchical structure. After she died, I felt no more attraction for the work and the hierarchical structure seemed dead to me. The people running it were continuing everything as if she were still there but to me the flavor that I was initially attracted to was gone.

I went through an intense time of doubting everything. It was very painful and there was nobody I could share it with. Krish was in a different place and felt threatened by my doubting and so I had to process this alone. It took me several months of doubting to finally decide to drop out of being a student at this mystery school. The school is very much like a club and dropping out meant saying good-bye to many acquaintances and maybe to friends. I didn't know if any of my friendships could survive my not being part of it any longer.

But I had to be true to myself. If I stayed it would be out of fear of losing friends or losing the sense of belonging, and I couldn't live with such a compromise. The deeper parts of me were calling me to break free, to not be part of any group or club or sect or anything but simply be me with everything that means. I felt that I needed to be with my own darkness rather than be in anybody's light and this was more important to me than anything else. I could not be a student of the people running the place.

So I dropped out. Krish continued to be part of it for another year and, at that time, was judging me for not wanting to be. He was mistrustful about my path, felt that maybe I didn't want to grow any longer and was copping out.

It opened up a deep wound in me to have the one I love not trust my way and even judge it. I believed that someone who loves me should understand me, support me, and should absolutely not judge anything that I do or decide. That someone who loves me should be behind me in every way. In Krish, I had found someone whom I felt very understood by, someone to share with, a real friend. And now this situation pulled the rug from under my feet. I felt so utterly betrayed and felt that I couldn't live with this kind of conditional love. At the same time, I was pulled back to him because I loved him and knew that I couldn't leave. My heart would not allow that. My mistrust voices were saying: "How can you love someone who doesn't support you and who even judges you?"

Being with the situation, feeling the pain and listening to these voices over and over, something inside me began to shift and I started realizing that it was not about him loving me unconditionally but about me loving myself enough to honor what I was going through. This situation presented me with an opportunity to honor and love myself enough to have the whole world against me or not understanding me, and still do what I felt was right. Somehow, I needed to go through this to realize that what I had been unconsciously demanding from Krish I needed to open up to inside myself.

There is never going to be anyone or anything outside that will ever be able to give that to me. It reflects a tremendous emptiness, loneliness, and sadness inside and only I can be with that and nourish it from the inside by not rejecting it. It was a test. It happened for my inner sense of direction to mature and for me to listen to it and stand up for it even if the whole world was against it. And I needed to go through this alone for the maturing to happen. At this point when I had come back to myself, Krish began to understand and see some of what I had been going through with this mystery school. I was now receiving the support and understanding that I had longed for from him, but it wasn't that important anymore and I could be there for him in his process of separating. The amazing thing is that a year later, Krish had a conflict with the people running the school and left after that. It presented him with his own process of separating from being part of the spiritual community that he had been with for over ten years. He had to go through a difficult time of feeling the grief of the loss of friends and community.

I now know that what I went through had nothing to do with the school or the other people. It was a test to stop projecting the support and understanding on the outside. It was a test to trust myself and in the direction life is taking me, even if at first I may not understand it or even if nobody on the outside understands it or supports it. It was a test of learning to follow that inner voice wherever it takes me and knowing that with that voice I cannot go wrong.

Exercise:

Ask yourself:

1. *Do I give my power away to authority? If so, what is my fear?*

2. *Am I able to strike a balance between opening to learn and trusting my own intuition and wisdom? Or do I go between compliance and rebellion?*

* * *

CHAPTER 15:

LIVING VERTICALLY –

Trusting Our Intelligence and Bringing Passion into Everyday Life

One of our biggest hurdles to being vital and trusting in life is a tendency to slip into living a life in which security, harmony, and resistance to growth rule our behavior and our way of looking at life. We call this "horizontal living."

In horizontal living, we are not trusting our own intelligence and we are not trusting life. In this frame of mind, we live in fear and are easily taken over by our regressed child. We don't stand up for ourselves, we minimize our needs, we build up secrets between us and those we love. We don't do what our heart is telling us to do and we don't speak our truth.

We allow practical details to take precedence over intimate sharing. We live in a state of diminished life energy, we compromise ourselves for approval and attention, and we give up vital aspects of our life to please another person. We stop making love or dealing with the issues that cause us to draw away sexually from the person we are intimate with. We can be so afraid of causing disharmony that we make all kinds of excuses not to say or do anything that could create disturbance.

We may even go so far as dealing with experiences of disappointment, frustration or betrayal by giving up on the person who disappoints us and eventually give up on love and life in general. Slowly, the relationship becomes distant and superficial until it dies. Or we may stay in a relationship which we know in our heart is over but we cannot find the courage to leave. Horizontal living creeps up on us in subtle ways. It makes our life and our relationships dusty, dry and stagnant. It can cause us to become deeply resigned and depressed. We may even notice that we are living a life much the same as our parents did, living the same old patterns, with very similar fears, habits, and routines and we have lost the joy and wonder of life.

Living a Vertical Lifestyle

If we introduce risk, energy, gratitude, and honesty into our life, we can begin to "live vertically." Our passion for truth, our passion of being fully alive, our passion of allowing life and other people to touch us deeply wakes up and we begin to live life with dignity and joy. When we are living vertically, our priorities change. We not only allow change, we welcome it, we begin to listen to our intuition and honor our life energy. We become less interested in what others think of us and more interested in following our heart in spite of the consequences.

Living vertically is a choice. It doesn't happen by itself. We all have a side of us that leans to the negative and another side of us that moves to the positive. When we choose to live vertically, we make a conscious choice to seek out people, experiences and activities that inspire the latter and choose to turn away from those that bring out our negativity.

The ingredients of vertical living include:

1. *Choosing and making the effort to spend time with people who inspire and honor us.*

2. *Including activities in our daily life that ignite our life energy.*

3. *Seeking guidance and new experiences that inspire us and help us to find ourselves.*

4. *Committing to being honest and to stop hiding in spite of our fears.*

5. *Standing up for ourselves and becoming less willing to compromise and prostitute ourselves.*

6. *Paying attention to any disturbances that develop with those close to us and making the effort to repair them up as they arise.*

7. *Choosing not to indulge obsessive thoughts that predictably bring on depression and decreased energy.*

8. *Accepting and even embracing that there are times in our life when there is sadness, loneliness, disappointment, and loss.*

9. *Taking regular small risks to discover, nurture, and express our creativity and live our dreams.*

10. *On an even broader perspective, surrendering to the natural flow of our life energy and beginning to live in tune with existence instead of fighting it.*

One very touching story we heard from a participant comes to mind. Maria was living at home with her parents. She began to become interested in the path of meditation and started to practice different meditations at home. Eventually, after some time, she went for a longer meditation retreat. When she returned from the retreat, her parents (traditional Italian Catholics) sat her down and told her that she had adopted a path of sin and unless she abandoned her new ways, they would cut her off financially and ask her to leave the house immediately. She spent a night of hell trying to decide what to do, but in the morning, she told her parents that she was leaving. Out on the street, devastated, without a job, a home, or any source of support, she had the presence of mind to sit down and write her priorities in a notebook.

She wrote, "First, I have to find a job. Second, I have to find a place to live. Third, I have to go back to the retreat place and continue my meditation, and finally, I need to study and work with what ignites my passion." She quickly found a job and a home and over the next several years found the time and the resources both to deepen her meditation practice and to take a training in "shiatsu," a form of bodywork that she had fallen in love with. She is still struggling to earn a living from her bodywork but she is persevering in spite of the obstacles.

When we take the first step toward vertical living, it is amazing how much existence supports us. Our fears will say that it is not possible to do what our heart wants to do and if we listen to those fears, it will not be possible. Many years ago, I (Krish) did a series of human potential trainings with an organization called Lifespring. One statement that one of the therapists made during one of those groups has stayed with me all these years: "When we argue for our limitations, they become ours."

When we are living horizontally, we are blocking the natural flow of life out of fear. When we are living vertically, we are willing to go through our fears, taking the risks our life energy is calling us to take and begin trusting our intuition. When we live vertically, we welcome any feelings, painful or pleasurable, opening up to them as a gift from existence. We stop the endless running after pleasure and we stop avoiding pain. Vertical living is living in trust; horizontal living is living in mistrust.

A friend of ours is living with a man she doesn't love. She complains that she is not in a fulfilling relationship and longs to be with someone who inspires her. When we suggest that until she leave the man she is with, there is no space in her life for another man to enter. Her response is, "I am too afraid to be alone and I don't like feeling lonely."

"What's wrong with feeling lonely?" we ask her.

"I don't want to feel lonely; I hate it."

We explain to her that unless she is willing to feel the loneliness and follow her heart, her wounded little girl is still leading her life. We suggest to her that she put her energy into her creativity and using her resources and intelligence to create a fulfilling life for herself. When loneliness comes, rather than running from the feelings, welcome and feel the emptiness and with time, the feeling will pass.

The Movement toward Living Vertically

Basically, it is an understanding and a passion for the truth that allows us to live vertically rather than horizontally. However, we can take some practical steps in our life that encourage this process. The movement toward living vertically requires risk. One such risk is the courage to separate from our family of origin, a topic that we have already given some attention to because we have learned that it is vital to our growth. When we stay bonded to those who raised us without making the effort to separate, we unconsciously take on their unconscious negativity and fears. Most of us came from environments that were horizontal, and this fear-based mentality will hold us back unless we break away from it. And even more importantly, when we stay bonded to our family of origin, we remain with the shame-based identity we received as a child, feeling unworthy and unloved, and through that it is very difficult to mature and find our own truth and intelligence.

Another important aspect of living vertically is learning to set limits, an issue that we have also discussed earlier. Several years ago I (Amana) came back to Denmark for a visit with my family. We went out for dinner at a restaurant and, as my mother is a high-profile businesswoman in town, she was nervous about our being there, particularly since the restaurant was owned by one of her customers and she wanted to make a good impression. To start the dinner I wanted a cup of tea and my mother was offended because as she said: "You don't have tea before your meal here in Denmark. Have a beer or a glass of wine." This was exactly the conditioning I was brought up with. "Don't do anything strange and abnormal."Only this time I had the strength and the courage to set the limit with her. I told her that I was going to have my cup of tea or I was leaving and never seeing them again. It was not OK for me that she told me what to do and not to do and that she had no right to interfere with my life and my decisions any longer. At that moment, I felt immense rage and at the same time was ready to take full responsibility for the consequences. I could not continue seeing her with that kind of interfering.

The most amazing thing happened. Her attitude changed, she apologized and shared what it was for her. She shared her fears of standing out and wanting to make a good impression in this restaurant. Hearing this something melted in me; we connected, and ever since then we have a very deep and close friendship. Now, when I look back on this incident, I have a different perspective. Now, I would still have had the cup of tea but I would also tell my mother how much I love her and respect her work and can understand her concern. At that time it was important to make a more dramatic stand as it was the first time I truly stood up to her in a direct way.

Living vertically can also involve reaching out for emotional and spiritual inspiration and guidance. It is easy to get locked into routine and low-energy states, to become bogged down with the practical details of life and to allow our minds and belief systems to become fixed.

Life Presents Us with Continual Challenges to Live Vertically

We are confronted with the choice of vertical or horizontal living all the time in our life. Sometimes it involves a major shift in our life such as ending a relationship that is no longer alive or leaving work that no longer suits us and finding something new, even if it means having less financial security. Sometimes, the challenges to live vertically are less dramatic situations but call on us to be more honest and open.

I (Krish) have a very close friend. We have known each other for over twenty years; we have shared the same spiritual master and lived together in a commune for many years. Now, we both live in Sedona. A few years ago, we had a major rift. We had been part of the same meditation community but I had a conflict with the people who were running the community and resigned. The breakup happened after a meeting where I felt betrayed and disrespected. My friend was there but remained silent during the discussion. I felt hurt that he did not stand up for me. I was not aware how hurt I actually was but I noticed that I started to pull away from him. I found myself judging him for being such a sissy and not having the courage to stand up for me and for continuing to be part of an organization that I felt was lacking in integrity.

I kept my judgments to myself but he knew how I was feeling. Finally one day, I decided to "come clean." We sat down and I shared my hurt, my disappointment, and my anger. He took his turn and shared his feelings. We cried. I got in touch with and shared the hurt and the betrayal I felt for his not supporting me at the meeting and for my feeling that he didn't understand my hurt. I told him that I had stopped trusting him as a friend because I felt that, of all people, I expected he should have stood up for me or at least understood how painful it was for me. But most importantly, I realized during our encounter that this whole experience had triggered a profound wound of betrayal and that he was only the catalyst for bringing up this pain. One of my deepest wounds has always been one of feeling unsupported. I was hurt because in the separation, I felt that I had lost one of my oldest and best friends and underneath my anger and distancing was a lot of hurt. Slowly over the weeks that followed our passionate and honest encounter, I noticed that something had profoundly changed inside of me in relation to him. My heart opened again. My judgments toward him had gone and his being a part of the community no longer seemed to interfere with my love for him. Paradoxically, a year later, he also quit.

The Quality of Life

In our work, we have a structure where we ask people to consider a risk that they might be willing to take to improve the quality of their life. We suggest five areas to explore:

1. *Toward a Loving Relationship of Body/Health*
2. *Toward a Functional Relating/Love/Connection*
3. *Toward a Fulfilling Creativity/Work/Finances*
4. *Toward a Healthy and Self-respecting Sexuality*
5. *Toward a Meaningful Spirituality*

At any time in our life, there is usually an area where we are being tested to expand, to live more vertically to increase our life energy. And increasing our quality of life will always require some kind of risk because our fears have held us back. So, we will need to encounter a fear. Perhaps we have a fear of rejection, of failure, of success, of disappointing someone, of having someone angry with us, or of breaking out of our comfort zone.

There are two sides of us. One side wants to stick with the familiar, the safe, the secure, and the known. But another side of us wants novelty, expansion, adventure, and growth. One side, which we call "the left side," holds our fear and our shame. The left also holds the body memory of traumas that we have received in the form to humiliations, judgments, criticism, invasions, and abandonments. So it is natural that we would be afraid of taking any kind of risk that might incur criticism, rejection, or judgments. Yet, the life force inside of us is strong. It is the strongest force there is. Between the force of fear and the force of life, life will win if we make even the smallest movement in its direction.

In the integration of our being, it is important to embrace the positive aspects of both sides and become conscious of the negatives aspects as well. The left, while holding our fears, inhibitions and shame, is also holds our vulnerability and our sensitivity. By welcoming and becoming intimately acquainted with this side, we learn compassion both for ourselves and for anyone who has known and experienced pain or difficulties. It brings us softness and gentleness. However, when not explored, felt, and embraced, it can lead to collapse, complaint, and a victim mentality. Or when we judge our or anyone else's vulnerability as weak, we can easily compensate by becoming tyrannical, irritated, pushy, impatient, and judgmental. This is the negative aspect of the right side.

Our growth as a person and living a more vertical life calls us to take risks on both sides.

Some of the possible risks on the right side can be:

1. *Expressing our creativity*
2. *Exercising our body*
3. *Learning to set limits*
4. *Becoming more honest with others*
5. *Eating in a more healthy way*
6. *Stopping self-destructive behaviors*
7. *Seeking guidance, direction and support*
8. *Coming out of isolation*
9. *Expressing our feelings and needs*

The possible risks on the left side could include:

1. *Creating more alone time and time that is not filled with structure and activity*

2. *Allowing ourselves to feel the fears and insecurities and seeking guidance to learn to do that*
3. *Making greater efforts to express our fears and insecurities to others especially those close to us*
4. *In general, opening to our softer side inside*

We are all different. Some of us have identified more strongly with our left side—with our vulnerability, fears, and insecurities. Others of us are much more focused on the right side—career oriented, being active, achieving, challenging ourselves and our bodies, engaging in sports, or spending a lot of time at work. It is interesting to notice what we value the most and that will help us see which side we are more identified with. Naturally, this is strongly affected by what we were taught were the important values in life.

> *When we value and are more focused on one side, most likely our risk toward growth will involve the opposite side.*

We were working recently with a couple who reflect this polarity quite strongly. The man was a highly successful businessman and had spent little time exploring or even interested in intimate relating or emotions. He had a tendency to be irritable, moody, impatient, and demanding, especially when he didn't get what he wanted. His wife, on the other hand, was more comfortable with her feelings and had been involved in spiritual and emotional growth for some time. She also had a tendency to please and placate him sacrificing her own needs and being a rescuer and caretaker. Their risks were quite different. His was to begin to feel the pain that he was carrying underneath his anger and control. Hers was to learn to set limits and to listen to her own needs.

Exercise:

Consider the five areas of your life mentioned above and ask yourself:

1. In what way am I not living my full potential in this area?

2. What is the fear if I would live fully in this area?

3. In what way would I be willing and able to make a small risk in this area?

* * *

CHAPTER 16:

INTEGRATION –

The Gradual Process of Becoming Human

Everything happens at its right moment.
Wait and watch.
Don't fall asleep – because in waiting,
that is very natural – to fall asleep.
You have to learn a meditative state of waiting.
It is very deep, a question of harmony.
Osho

Integration comes with a deep quality of acceptance—acceptance for who we are, acceptance for our shortcomings, our
imperfections and for all that happened to us in the past that
brought pain and fear. It comes with an acceptance of whatever we
did out of unawareness that caused pain to other people. Integration does not mean that we stop growing, we will be growing until
we die, but it does mean that we begin to let go of striving to be different, striving for a goal, for change, for improvement, for higher
states of consciousness. Once we begin to accept who we are, we
become more human, more reachable, more relaxed, and softer.

We use a structure in one of our workshops in which we explore what makes a person attractive to members of the opposite sex. We have been using this structure for many years and what we find is very interesting. Paradoxically, what makes a person attractive has nothing to do with physical beauty or image. It seems to be based on how much he or she is resting in him or herself with ease and self-acceptance—how much this person is willing to be with whatever is happening and not cover up insecurity or fear

When I (Krish) first started on this journey of awakening, I was very much focused on "getting there"—on changing my consciousness, on getting free of my ego and becoming a fully awakened being. And in the beginning, I expected and experienced dramatic changes—in my sense of self, my life energy and my ability to feel and be open. But over time, the changes became less and less obvious and detectable. I began to see that my ego and my defenses were not going to dissolve as quickly as I hoped and neither were my fears and insecurities. I was forced to adapt myself to the reality that change is often discouragingly slow. The process of opening and trusting seems to be extremely subtle and gradual and it is one that often lacks tangible results and has frequent setbacks. I have also had to make peace with those parts of myself that I didn't like.

Learning to Live without Expectations

At any given moment on our journey, it can be difficult to appreciate the changes that are happening because we are too identified with ourselves and don't have the distance to see clearly. And in moments of setback or when mistrust takes over, our inner judge becomes powerfully harsh and critical because many of us have high standards for ourselves. When we get hit with a shame attack, a rejection, a loss, when we notice ourselves behaving in ways we don't like or have uncomfortable feelings such as irritation, rage, sadness or boredom, we can easily feel that nothing has changed.

We may feel that we are as negative, angry, and frustrated, useless, deflated, or disturbed as we have ever been.

Recently, two clients of ours, who have worked with us for years, wrote to us in much pain and hopelessness. After entering into promising love stories, their boyfriends left and went back to their former girlfriends. They both felt that they have been working so intensively with themselves, looking at their patterns and feeling the pain even to the point that there were no tears left and simply could not understand why nothing had changed. The same old thing was happening again—being rejected by men that they had opened to and felt some trust with. They were asking us what else could they possibly do? What more inner work was there to do? When does it end? When will the love finally come? Was there something that they were doing wrong? Is there something terribly wrong with them that this keeps happening?

One of the mistakes many of us make is to think that when we do the work intensely, feel our pain, go through the grief, then we are going to get rewarded—for example, by some magical love story. If we are doing the work hoping and expecting to get a certain result then we are still living horizontally. Then it is our regressed child waiting for the reward and getting disappointed when it doesn't happen according to our desires. Life does not work that way. There are no guarantees that love is going to come into our life and shower us with blessings now that we feel ready. All any of us can do is simply to open up to whatever existence wants to show us, give us and teach us. All we can do is to stop fighting and to begin enjoying the beauty of what is—to let go of our ideas about how things should be and simply take in life with all its pain and pleasure.

Most of the time, changes in our consciousness, our relating and our self-esteem are microscopic, and if we focus on a goal, we will miss them and lose heart. It is important to be aware of the small changes in our life and to accept that at times, we will regress and find ourselves back to feeling much the same way we felt in the past.

Embracing the Dark Side

Embracing our woundedness can seem easy compared to embracing the dark parts of our personality—those parts we don't like—such as our negativity, dishonesty, viciousness, anger, vengefulness, competitiveness, and defensiveness. It helps to understand that these dark parts of us are not some basic defects in our being but they simply come from a deep mistrust of people and of life. These behaviors and ways of thinking were survival mechanisms born out of panic and hurts that we accumulated over a very long time. We had many years to become convinced that this was the only way to survive and when our survival feels threatened, we resort to all kinds of strategies. To the child inside, it is a matter of life and death when our betrayal wound has been triggered.

It is hard not to judge this part of us. But when we judge something, we don't have the space to be present to it. I (Krish) have a strong tyrannical and judgmental side of me. I don't like it but it is there. All the male members of my family have had this quality and I inherited it as well. It is one thing for me to see this energy arise when I am in a safely contained environment as a participant in a therapy session or a group but it is quite another when it comes up in my everyday life. Then the behaviors and feelings are more difficult to accept precisely because I see how damaging and hurtful they can be. I can't imagine how anyone could love me when I show this part of me and it feels horribly "unevolved." But repressing it or pretending it isn't there only makes it come out indirectly. Then, it attracts my attention in judgments, criticism, moodiness, irritability, and blame. I am learning to accept it by knowing where it comes from and, when I remember, to connect with the hurt underneath. Befriending our primitive rage is an ongoing process for many of us.

Giving Love a Higher Priority than Being Right

In some ways, our relationships are the most accurate mirror of our level of maturity and trustfulness and the arena where we can get the most practice. In the area of our work and creativity, it is easier to hide our lack of integration behind the blaze of talent and the energy of ambition and drive. And if our focus in life has been on accomplishment, it is not uncommon to excel in this department without realizing how little we have integrated in the deeper aspects of our being. We can be wealthy, powerful, and unsurpassed in our work and impoverished, lonely, and unfulfilled in our ability to remain connected and open with another person.

In our work and in our less intimate connections, we can remain fixed in old identities, defenses and modes of behavior without it creating too much of a problem. When work and achievement comes first, the openness and flow of interpersonal relating can take a backseat, and it often does. But in our love life, we simply cannot stick to our old habits and expect love, trust and nourishment to continue. If we do, the love that was there initially will die.

> *In life, nothing is ever static. Life energy is continually moving and flowing. If the love and intimacy is not deepening and strengthening then it means that it is becoming shallower and weaker, and it takes some committed work to consciously open again to deeper levels of vulnerability.*

I (Amana) notice that I very easily can move into a space of simply doing my own things where I am very comfortable but there is no deep connection to Krish or anyone else. This is a place that is highly developed in me and is a place of hiding. I had to find this place early in life, as there was no one to connect with emotionally. It takes conscious effort for me to come out of my own inner sanctuary and actually connect. And it takes a lot for me to open up and share myself. My child inside is always checking to see if it is safe enough to be vulnerable and if the other person has the space for that.

> *Integrating shows itself in our relating arena as we find ourselves more able to place love higher than needing to be right or in control. It shows itself when we start to take responsibility and look inside rather than running automatically into blame.*

As we mature, we find the ability to choose love over conflict and control because we already know where certain of our behaviors lead to and we have gotten sick of the same old scenario. As we mature, we just don't have the same need to be right. Compared to feeling love, feeling right feels quite trivial. And most importantly, we stop relying on the other person to fulfill us. We are more able to be with ourselves and to be OK with ourselves even when the other is not available or frustrates us in some way.

Integration brings the ability to contain frustration. When we learn to contain frustration and pain, it is not necessary to process every small incident with the other person. Processing and communication of hurts is important and certainly a preferred alternative to repressing and moving into cold resentment. But as more inner space grows, we can let things go while in the past we might have felt we needed to react or process. Bear in mind though, that we are not talking about repression here. This is a very important distinction and can easily be misunderstood.

Our regressed child will probably always be reactive and defensive. But gradually, we gain greater ability to notice our hurt and reactiveness with some distance. With time, we seem to get more choice between reacting in our old ways or choosing new ways to being with ourselves when we are triggered by something. As the space inside grows, we have a choice to being with the discomfort of our emotions instead of blindly reacting. We gain distance from the old ways of blaming, cutting off, and isolating, feeling silently hurt but not expressing ourselves. With time, we get to see that these old ways are like dark roads that we have been down countless times in the past and we know that they only go into deeper isolation, hurt, or escalating conflict. So, we become motivated to work with different ways to respond to hurt and irritation. Old ways don't vanish so quickly, but as we integrate, we start to pick something new. Gratitude grows for the nourishment that we are getting.

The experience of a very close friend of ours comes to mind. He has been with a woman for ten years. Up until a year ago, he would chronically complain about her being too speedy, too childish, too reactive, etc. etc. etc…It got so boring to hear and be with. I (Krish) finally told him that I just couldn't hear it anymore. It was not helpful for him to discover the childhood roots of his complaining—he had done plenty of that. Then something changed. He made a choice to move into gratitude. And it worked. Instead of feeding his complaining mind, he gave energy to how much he appreciated his beloved. Soon, it became easy for him to feel how much he respected and loved her in spite of all the qualities that he complained about before. In fact, even those qualities became lovable. Almost miraculously, during this period, their creative life blossomed as well. They share a ceramics business and he was also developing his skills as a painter.

Developing the Emotional Ground to Face the Abyss

There is a story about a man who fell off a cliff into a vast abyss. As he was falling, he grabbed a branch to break his fall and then was hanging from this branch for his life.

Looking up to the sky, he shouted, "Is there anyone up there who can help me?"

A voice, booming from the heavens, responded, "Let go!"

The man thought about it for a moment and said, "Is there anyone else up there?"

For years, our spiritual master spoke to us about learning to face the void. He taught us and showed us through meditations that we are essentially naked and that all our possessions, loved ones, identities, and doings cannot hide this fact. No matter what we do, we cannot avoid confronting this space. The things that we rely on for meaning have to fall away because they are unsubstantial. It is one thing to hear these words and even understand them in deep meditation and it is quite another to integrate their meaning into daily life. Normally, we prop ourselves up with career, children, substances, activity, and a sense of identity that gives us meaning.

As long as we can stay busy with these activities and as long as the identity holds meaning for us, we don't have to confront our emptiness. Perhaps we can't see through the shields that we construct in order not to have to confront this void until we have an accident, lose a job, have a large financial setback, or suffer a profound loss or illness. But somewhere in the background of our awareness is an inner knowing of the truth of the void that we are constantly avoiding. In some ways, opening to feeling the void is our deepest test of trust. How can we find the inner space to go into this with trustfulness that it will open us to a deeper wisdom and not swallow us up?

The emotional strength we need to face our emptiness comes from facing our fears and our buried pain, honestly and sincerely. As that develops, we move gradually into seeing through our veils of illusion. Our regressed child does not want nor have the space to feel or see this. But somewhere inside, we know that our ego identities are just castles of sand.

Recently, we were doing a session with a couple and one of the issues that came up was the woman's problem with alcohol as well as a history of sexual abuse. She said that she drank because she felt such a profound emptiness inside and it helped her to deal with the violence and emptiness in the world and between people. The alcohol and other ways that she acted out from fear was sabotaging the love between them. She entered a treatment program and began working a Twelve-Step Program. Simultaneously, she worked weekly with a therapist trained to work with sexual abuse issues. Not only was she able to stop drinking but she was also able to face the fears that she had been avoiding to feel. Up until then, she was not ready to work a program or face these fears. She had tried in the past without success. But this time, she was ready. Her life has changed dramatically. She feels stronger and has self-esteem for the first time in her life.

When we see life through the eyes of our traumatized child, going deeper into feeling our inner void seems like a nightmare without end. However, when we go deeply inside and are willing to feel and allow our pain and fears, we naturally begin to reconnect with our strength, our grounding and our self-love. This begins to build an inner sense of strength and connectedness that becomes the foundation which we need to face the emptiness. And through that emptiness, we can connect with real trust, a trust that is not dependent on anything on the outside but grounded in our being and our connection to existence.

Exercise:

Ask yourself:

What in my life am I grateful for?

1. *In my relationships?*

2. *My health and body?*

3. *My gifts and natural talents?*

4. *My children and my parents?*

* * *

CONCLUSION

We are constantly learning what it means to live in trust.

Working with people is a great privilege because it forces us to keep looking, to keep questioning, and to keep making every effort to stay honest with ourselves and with others. Sometimes when we are teaching, we hear things come out of our mouths and we wonder where the heck that came from. Many times, when we are talking to a group of people, it feels like we are also talking to ourselves.

In conclusion, in our experience, the quality of trust comes because of a deep soul searching. It does not depend on the behavior and qualities of another person, or on how life treats us. It depends on how deeply we have learned to trust ourselves. To trust, we have to trust our trust.

We would like to end by sharing with you a short but inspiring quote from our teacher:

> *Each individual should have a direct contact with the universe, its beauty, its tremen-*

dous glory – which creates, without any effort, a gratitude, a prayer, perhaps a song, a dance…

I stand for the individual…

But this needs a tremendous courage to revolt and assert your individuality, whatever the consequences.

You have to learn to love yourself first, to respect yourself first. And then certainly it will give you tremendous nourishment and it will start spreading around you.

Osho

* * *

SELECTED REFERENCES

Banks, Coleman *Birdsong, Fifty-three Short Poems by Rumi*. Maypop, 1993

Bradshaw, John. *Creating Love – The Next Stage of Growth*. New York: Bantam Books, 1992

Brown, Byron. *Soul Without Shame – A Guide to Liberating Yourself from the Judge Within.* Shambala, 1999

Chopra, Deepak. Ed. *The Love Poems of Rumi.* Harmony Books, 1998

Deida, David. *It's a Guy's Thing – An Owner's Manual for Women*, Health Communications, Inc. 1997

Deida, David. *Intimate Communion – Awakening Your Sexual Essence* Health Communications, Inc. 1995

Firestone, Robert W. *The Fantasy Bond – The Structure of Psychological Defenses.* The Glenstone Association, 1987

Hendrix, Harville, PhD. *Getting the Love You Want.* New York: Henry Holt and Co., 1998, 2008

Hellinger, Bert. *Touching Love.* Phoenix: Carl-Auer-System Publishing, 1997

Herman, Judith. *Trauma and Recovery - The Aftermath of Violence from Domestic Abuse to Political Terror.* New York: Basic Books, 1992

Karen, Robert, PhD. *Becoming Attached – First Relationships and How They Shape Our Capacity to Love.* New York: Oxford University Press, 1998

Kohut, Heinz. *Restoration of the Self,* International Universities Press, 1977

Lerner, Rokelle. *Living in the Comfort Zone – The Gift of Boundaries in Relationships.* Health Communications, Inc., 1995

Levine, Stephen and Ondrea. *Embracing the Beloved – Relationship as a Path of Awakening.* Anchor Books, 1995

Levine, Peter with Ann Frederick *Waking the Tiger – Healing Trauma.* North Atlantic, Books 1997

Levine, Peter. *Healing Trauma – A Pioneering Program for Restoring the Wisdom of Your Body.* Boulder, CO: Sounds True, 2005

Long, Barry. *Making Love – Sexual Love the Divine Way.* Barry Long Books, 1998

Mellody, Pia. *Facing Love Addiction – Giving Yourself the Power to Change the Way You Love.* HarperCollins Publishers, 1992

Mellody, Pia. *The Intimacy Factor – The Ground Rules for Overcoming the Obstacles to Truth, Respect, and Lasting Love.* San Francisco: Harper, 2004

Maitri, Sandra. *The Spiritual Dimension of the Enneagram – Nine Faces of the Soul.* Tarcher/Putnam 2000

Mate, Gabor MD. *Scattered Minds – A New Look at the Origins and Healing of Attention Deficit Disorder.* Toronto, 2000

Miller, Alice. *The Drama of the Gifted Child - The Search for the True Self.* Basic Books, l976

Osho. *Om Mane Padme Om.* Rebel Publikations 1987

Osho. *Zarathustra, The God That Can Dance – Commentaries on Friedrich Nietzsche's Thus Spoke Zarathustra.* Rebel Publishing, 1987

Osho. *Zarathustra, The Laughing Prophet – Commentaries on Friedrich Nietzsche's Thus Spoke Zarathustra,* Rebel Publications, 1987

Pierrakos, Eva and Thesenga, Donovan. *Fear No Evil, The Pathwork Method of Transforming The Lower Self.* Pathworks Press 199

Rothchild, Babette. *The Body Remembers – The Psychophysiology of Trauma and Trauma Treatment.* New York: W. W. Norton and Co. , 2000

Rosenberg, Marshall B. PhD. *Nonviolent Communication – A Language of Life.* Encinitas, CA: Puddle Dancer Press, 2003

Shapiro, Francine PhD, and Forrest, Margot Silk. *EMDR – Eye Movement Desensitization and Reprocessing.* New York: Basic Books, 1997

Stone, Hal, PhD & Stone, Sidra L. *Partnering – A New Kind of Relationship.* Novato, CA: New World Library, 2000

Subby, Robert. *Lost in the Shuffl - The Co-Dependent Reality.* Heal Communications, Inc. l987

Wallin, David, J. *Attachment in Psychotherapy.* New York: The Guilford Press, 2007

Weinhold, Janae B. PhD & Weinhold, Barry K. PhD. *The Flight From Intimacy – Healing Your Relationships of Counter-dependency – the Other Side of Co-dependency.* Novato, CA: New World Library, 2007

Wolinsky, Stephen PhD. *The Way of the Human Volume II – The False Core and the False Self.* Quantum Institute, 1999

Made in the USA
Middletown, DE
18 November 2019